Greek Lyric Metre

Greek Lyric Metre

BY

GEORGE THOMSON, M.A.

FELLOW AND LECTURER OF KING'S COLLEGE
AND FORMERLY CRAVEN STUDENT IN THE
UNIVERSITY OF CAMBRIDGE

CAMBRIDGE

AT THE UNIVERSITY PRESS

1929

CAMBRIDGE
UNIVERSITY PRESS

University Printing House, Cambridge CB2 8BS, United Kingdom

Published in the United States of America by Cambridge University Press, New York

Cambridge University Press is part of the University of Cambridge.

It furthers the University's mission by disseminating knowledge in the pursuit of education, learning and research at the highest international levels of excellence.

www.cambridge.org
Information on this title: www.cambridge.org/9781107690141

© Cambridge University Press 1929

First published 1929
First paperback edition 2013

A catalogue record for this publication is available from the British Library

ISBN 978-1-107-69014-1 Paperback

TO MY MOTHER

PREFACE

THE English reader does not need to make a detailed study of the rules of versification in order to enjoy English poetry. He can recognise blank verse, or the sonnet, or the heroic couplet, when he meets it, and for the rest he can safely trust his ear to guide him. But with Greek poetry it is different. The Greek convention is foreign to him, and more elaborate than his own. He reads a piece of Aeschylean lyric, for example. Parts of it seem quite straightforward; they appeal to his instinct for rhythm and, although he might find it no easy matter to analyse them, he is satisfied. Other parts are not so simple—he succeeds, with difficulty, in getting some sort of rhythm out of them, but he is not at all sure that it is the right rhythm. And in other parts again he feels that he is altogether astray. This is a serious obstacle to his enjoyment of Greek poetry.

The first business of the student of Greek metre should be to remove this obstacle; and much has been done in this direction by German scholars—Wilamowitz, Schröder, and others—in the last quarter of a century. Discarding the arbitrary preconceptions of their predecessors and the Procrustean methods with which they contorted the facts to fit them, and relying on what is best and most authoritative in ancient tradition, these scholars succeeded in clearing away many difficulties and in illuminating much that was formerly obscure. Not only have they shown the modern reader how to distinguish the various types of Greek rhythm, but they have given him a general idea of the smaller elements—the phrases—without doing violence to his ear.

Much, however, still remains to be done. Granted that this passage is in one rhythm and that in another, that this phrase is Glyconic and that "iambo-choriambic," why, the reader may fairly ask, does one rhythm give place, within the compass of a single poem, or even of a single strophe, to another, why does iambo-choriambic follow Glyconic and yield in turn to choriambic, with such bewildering unexpectedness? Is there any rhyme or reason in it at all?

The first scholar to tackle this problem was the late Walter Headlam. He showed, in the first place, that these transitions are not arbitrary or abrupt; that, in the hands of the Greek poet, one rhythm grows out of another, naturally and beautifully, in accordance with a few rhythmical laws so simple that anyone with an ear for rhythm can understand them. And in the second place, not content with explaining *how* these transitions were effected, he went on to enquire *why*, and discovered that certain rhythms tended to be associated with certain ideas, thus laying the foundations for a theory of *significant* rhythm.

Unhappily, Headlam did not live to complete the work he had begun; and the only monument of his metrical discoveries that he has left behind him is his brief, but brilliant, article in the *Journal of Hellenic Studies*[1]. Naturally, it was impossible for him to prove to others, within the compass of that article, that his principles stood the test of application to all the facts, though those who are familiar with Headlam's scholarship can have little doubt that he had proved it to himself. The primary object of this book is to show that they do stand this test, that not only do they remove obstacles from the path of the reader who wishes to read Greek lyric poetry with pleasure and discernment, but they bring to light new beauties which have hitherto lain unsuspected.

Therefore it is my application of Headlam's theory, rather than the theory itself, that is new. At the same time, it will be seen that I have developed his theory in certain important directions along lines indicated by him but not followed up. For the sake of completeness I have incorporated his work into my own, with acknowledgments where they are due, but

---

[1] *J.H.S.* vol. XXII (1902), pp. 209-27.

the reader who is interested in the subject will find it helpful,
I think, to study Headlam's article in conjunction with this
book.

Further, I must mention my debt to Mr J. T. Sheppard, who
taught me the right method of approach to the study of Greek
poetical technique. Some of his work has been published, and
to that I shall refer in the proper place, but most of it has
been conveyed to me through the more intimate channels of
college teaching, and for that no reference can be given, nor
any adequate acknowledgment.

Lastly, I wish to thank Professor D. S. Robertson for cor-
recting some mistakes and for several helpful suggestions.

GEORGE THOMSON

CAMBRIDGE, *January*, 1929

NOTE

References:

> To the lyric poets (except Bacchylides): Bergk, *Poetae Lyrici Graeci*
> (vol. I, 1900; vol. II, 1915; vol. III, 1914), also Diehl, *Anthologia
> Lyrica*, 1922-5 (in the Index).
> To Bacchylides: Jebb, 1905.
> To Aeschylus: Wecklein, 1885.
> To Sophocles: Pearson, 1924.
> To Euripides: Murray, 1902-13.

CONTENTS

CHAPTER ONE

POETRY AND MUSIC

THE arts of poetry and music, sprung from a common mother—the dance—are sisters; but their relations to each other have not always been the same. In modern Europe they are almost entirely independent; poets require no knowledge of music, nor musicians of poetry. And when the two consent to collaborate, it is usually on the strict understanding that music shall be mistress. In the Wagnerian ideal of grand opera, music, poetry and dancing were to be harmoniously combined—music supreme, supported by the other two. Similarly, in setting a poem to music, the modern composer is not usually concerned to heighten the value of the piece as poetry; his object is rather to adapt the poet's idea to a new artistic form, and in pursuit of that object he does not scruple to abandon the natural rhythm and melody of the poetry in favour of a new rhythm and melody of his own.

This form of song, in which music is the dominant, poetry the subordinate, element, has not prevailed in every age. Listening to an Elizabethan song, we feel that the two are more evenly balanced. The music is simple; it does not defy, but enforces and amplifies, the rhythm of the poetry. The poetry is also simple, and so lends itself the more readily to musical accompaniment. Turning to the ancient Greek convention, we find yet a further difference. The greater part of Greek poetry, outside didactic verse and dramatic dialogue, was written expressly for musical accompaniment: even Homer may, like his own Demodocus, have sung to the lyre. Moreover, if poetry and music commonly went hand in hand, there was no question but that poetry was the mistress and music the handmaid. We know little of Greek music, but what we know confirms this view. There was no harmony; the choir sang in unison to the accompaniment often of a single instrument—sometimes to the lyre and flute combined. The words of the singer were the dominant element, and often reached, both in sense and in rhythm, a degree of elaboration rarely equalled in the poetry of other ages. The music which accompanied such poetry was necessarily simple. The age of which I am speaking is the great lyrical period, from its inauguration by Terpander to its culmination in Aeschylus and Pindar and in the earlier work of Sophocles. Already, in the fifth century, a change was setting in; but the evidence for this change only confirms what has been said of the earlier period. Thus Pratinas, a contemporary of Aeschylus, complains of certain musical innovations in the form of the choral dance known as the hyporcheme. He declares that the flute is no longer made to follow the singer, but the singer the flute[1].

Τίς ὁ θόρυβος ὅδε; τί τάδε τὰ χορεύματα;
τίς ὕβρις ἔμολεν ἐπὶ Διονυσιάδα πολυπάταγα θυμέλαν;

The rhythm of this apparently incoherent succession of short syllables cannot be determined without the aid of the music which accompanied it. Having thus playfully imitated the new-fangled style of which he disapproves, Pratinas goes on to explain what the flute-player's proper business is:

τὰν ἀοιδὰν κατέστασε Πιερὶς βασίλειαν· ὁ δ' αὐλὸς
ὕστερον χορευέτω· καὶ γάρ ἐσθ' ὑπηρέτας.

'The song is mistress, the music her handmaid.' And with these words, set to a rhythm that is unmistakable, Pratinas returns to the more seemly practice of his ancestors.

But younger poets were not deterred by this protest from carrying their innovations into tragedy itself. In many of the choral songs of Euripides, we feel that the author is writing

---

[1] Bergk III (pp. 557-9); Athen. xiv 617B Πρατίνας δὲ ὁ Φλιάσιος αὐλητῶν καὶ χορευτῶν μισθοφόρων κατεχόντων τὰς ὀρχήστρας, ἀγανακτεῖν τινας ἐπὶ τῷ τοὺς αὐλητὰς μὴ συναυλεῖν τοῖς χοροῖς, καθάπερ ἦν πάτριον, ἀλλὰ τοὺς χοροὺς συνᾴδειν τοῖς αὐληταῖς· ὃν οὖν εἶχε θυμὸν κατὰ τῶν ταῦτα ποιούντων ὁ Πρατίνας ἐμφανίζει διὰ τοῦδε τοῦ ὑπορχήματος. Plato agreed with Pratinas: Rep. iii 398 D καὶ μὴν τήν γε ἁρμονίαν καὶ ῥυθμὸν ἀκολουθεῖν δεῖ τῷ λόγῳ.

for an audience which is more intent on following his music than his poetry. The words are weak and sometimes repeated without regard to the sense for the sake of the musical accompaniment, much in the manner of the modern song.

Eur. *Or.* 1414–17

περὶ δὲ γόνυ χέρας ἱκεσίους ἔβαλον ἔβαλον Ἑλένας ἄμφω.
ἀνὰ δὲ δρομάδες ἔθορον ἔθορον ἀμφίπολοι Φρύγες.

The Aeschylus of the *Frogs* ridicules Euripides for writing in this new-fangled style:

Ar. *Ran.* 1353–5

ἐμοὶ δ᾽ ἄχε᾽ ἄχεα κατέλιπε,
δάκρυα δάκρυά τ᾽ ἀπ᾽ ὀμμάτων
ἔβαλον ἔβαλον ἁ τλάμων.

If we may trust the same critic, Euripides did not stop there. His music sometimes broke right away from the rhythm of the words, which was contorted to fit the unnatural pattern:

Ibid. 1346–8

ἐγὼ δ᾽ ἁ τάλαινα προσέχουσ᾽ ἔτυχον
ἐμαυτῆς ἔργοισι,
λίνου μεστὸν ἄτρακτον
εἰειειειλίσσουσα χεροῖν....

No doubt, Aristophanes is exaggerating; but the fact that such a parody was possible shows that, in the hands of Euripides, the music was becoming more, and the poetry less, important, and that these tendencies were new.

The full effect of Greek choral lyric is irrecoverable, because of the three elements which made up that composite art only the poetry survives. We can still hear the words of the poet; but his lyre is dumb, and the feet of his dancers have vanished. We may, however, console ourselves with the knowledge that the one element we possess was, at least in the earlier period, the most important of the three. Down to the middle of the fifth century, the flute-player played, and the dancer danced, in time with the natural rhythm of the poetry.

Once this is granted, the task of analysing the extant

remains of Greek metre becomes very much simpler. If we may assume that the rhythm of the music followed the rhythm of the words, then the surest way of discovering the metre of a piece of Greek lyric is to read it according to the sense. Recite it aloud, marking the natural pauses and word-groupings, the climaxes and the cadences, which the sense of the words dictates to the understanding, and the ear will grasp the rhythm. Moreover, since we possess in the words the rhythmical element of the musical accompaniment, by examining them we may hope to discover something of the nature of Greek music. Most students of that subject have concentrated their attention on the melody—a problem beset with difficulties; they have tended to overlook the easier method of approach— the rhythm of the words preserved in our texts.

All that is required to grasp the principles of Greek metre is a sense of rhythm and of poetry. A knowledge of modern music will make the task still easier. Since Pindar was a musician as well as a poet, we must remember that, while the sense and emotional value of his words is always his first consideration, he will tend to use his rhythms as a musician uses them. Music has developed, in the last two centuries, into an art different in many respects from the music of any other period; but it has preserved the fundamental qualities characteristic of the music of all ages. If we can isolate these, sifting the universal from the particular, we shall be entitled to avail ourselves of what light they may throw on the study of Greek metre; and I venture to predict that our method will be justified by its results.

We must begin, however, with an account, as simple as possible, of the verse or phrase, and of the feet of which it is composed. We will pass on to the group of phrases, or sentence; and so, working our way through the strophe and the triad, we will conclude our enquiry with some account of the poem as a whole—the single Pindaric ode, and the dramatic stasimon, which must be considered in relation to the still larger units of the play and the trilogy.

CHAPTER TWO

THE PHRASE

Dear harp of my country, in dark - ness I
found thee, the cold chain of silence had hung o'er thee long.[1]

THE smallest rhythmical units into which this piece of music may be divided are the bars, which mark the disposition of the recurrent beats or accents. But they give no indication of the rhythm of the passage as a whole :

Dear / harp of my / country, in / darkness I / found thee, the / cold chain of / silence had / hung o'er thee / long.

A better clue is provided by the four figures or sections, which are independent of the bars :

> Dear harp of my country,
> In darkness I found thee,
> The cold chain of silence
> Had hung o'er thee long.

Even that, however, is not entirely satisfactory. As we listen to the song, we feel that the first two figures, and the last two, should be taken together :

> Dear harp of my country, in darkness I found thee,
> The cold chain of silence had hung o'er thee long.

These are phrases—the smallest units which are sufficiently self-contained to convey an adequate impression of the rhythm

---

[1] See Stewart Macpherson, *Form in Music*, pp. 9-10, from which this example is taken.

The same principle holds good in English prosody. Take any piece of versification, the simpler the better:

> Of all the girls that are so smart
> There's none like pretty Sally.

We may, if we like, divide these lines into feet: Of all / the girls / that are / so smart / there's none / like pret/. . . and so on. But it does not help much, because, if we want to grasp the rhythm, we must attend, not to the individual feet, but to the verse as a whole. So in Greek:

Ar. *Ach. 836*

εὐδαιμονεῖ γ᾽ ἄνθρωπος. οὐκ ἤκουσας οἳ προβαίνει . . .

This passage may be divided into feet (iambi and spondees), or into two figures (–́ ᴗ́ –́ ᴗ́ and –́ ᴗ́ ᴗ́–), but the vital rhythmical unit consists of these two figures taken together—the verse or phrase.

We shall look to the phrase, therefore, rather than to the feet of which it is composed, as the organic unit of measurement in Greek metre, and in this we shall be justified by the principles underlying prosody and music alike. In the case of Greek metre, moreover, there is a further reason why we should adopt this method. The phrase is immediately apprehended by the ear, the bar or foot only by a more conscious process of analysis. Now, in modern music we can always find out how the phrases are barred, if our ears cannot do it for us, by reference to the score. But the scores of Greek music have perished; and though we can grasp the unity of the phrase as a whole, we do not always know how it was divided into bars—indeed, we cannot be sure that it was barred, in the modern sense, at all.

The modern composer invents his phrases as he goes along. Bound by no convention, he gives free rein to his fancy, and the only authority to which he owes obedience is his ear. So, to some extent, with the Greek poet; he too is at liberty to invent phrases of his own if he pleases. At the same time, he possesses in common with his audience a large stock of phrases which have become stereotyped by constant usage; and it is out of these elements that he constructs the framework of most of his rhythmical designs.

Our first business, therefore, will be to identify and classify the various phrases admitted by common convention. For the present we will content ourselves with noticing only the most frequent; once these have been grasped, the rest will be acquired without difficulty in the subsequent stages of our enquiry. The Greek poet recognised four classes of rhythm, each of which contains a number of these standard phrases. The simplest, and one of the most important, is the rhythm which most modern metricians call dactylo-epitrite; but we will study it under the less formidable name which Headlam gave it[1]—Dorian.

Dorian phrases are built up of two figures : one is dactylic, DORIAN the other is called the epitrite, and may be represented by the symbol ∸ ◡ ∸ –[2].

Pind. *O*. iii 1

Τυνδαρίδαις τε φιλοξείνοις ἀδεῖν καλλιπλοκάμῳ θ' Ἑλένᾳ.

Here we have two such dactylic phrases, with an epitrite between them. They are called prosodiacs, and normally consist of two dactyls followed by a spondee, as in the first example (weak ending), or by a single long syllable, as in the second (strong ending). Sometimes they contain three dactyls, and sometimes only one. Similarly, the epitrite consists of a trochee followed either by a spondee, or by a single long (∸ ◡ ∸). And here again we sometimes find a longer form, with two trochees instead of one (∸◡ ∸◡ ∸ –). Finally, in both

---

[1] W. Headlam, *J.H.S.* vol. XXII, p. 212.

[2] Whether the Greeks recognised a rhythmical beat, or *ictus*, is not certain (see J. M. Edmonds, *Lyra Graeca*, III, pp. 587–9) : but the modern reader will find it easier to distinguish between the various Greek rhythms if he assumes that they did. I have therefore marked the rhythmical beat on those syllables where, to an English ear, it would naturally fall.

prosodiac and epitrite the final spondee may be represented by a trochee : ‒ ∪ ∪ ‒ ∪ ∪ ‒◡ and ‒∪ ‒◡.

The typical Dorian phrase is made up of these two figures combined in various ways. In the following example, each verse represents a phrase, and ought always to be printed as such, while the component figures are marked off by horizontal lines :

Aesch. *P. V.* 542–51

μηδάμ' ὁ πάντα νέμων θεῖτ' ἐμᾷ γνώμᾳ κράτος ἀντίπαλον Ζεύς,
μηδ' ἐλινύσαιμι θεοὺς ὁσίαις θοίναις ποτινισσομένα
βουφόνοις παρ' Ὠκεανοῦ πατρὸς ἄσβεστον πόρον,
μηδ' ἀλίτοιμι λόγοις, ἀλλά μοι τόδ' ἐμμένοι καὶ μήποτ' ἐκτακείη.

IONIAN   Our second class of rhythm is called Ionian, and its most characteristic phrases are built up out of the foot called Ionic a minore (∪ ∪ ‒ ‒), which will be familiar to readers of Horace :

Hor. *Od.* iii 12

Miserarum est neque amori dare ludum...

Aesch. *Pers.* 88–91

δόκιμος δ' οὔτις ὑποστὰς μεγάλῳ ῥεύματι φωτῶν
ἐχυροῖς ἔρκεσιν εἴργειν ἄμαχον κῦμα θαλάσσης.

A slight change in the rhythmical accent will give us, instead of Ionic a minore (∪ ∪ ‒ ‒), another rhythm : ‒ ∪ ∪ ‒. This is choriambic :

Soph. *O. T.* 483–4

δεινὰ μὲν οὖν δεινὰ ταράσσει σοφὸς οἰωνοθέτας.

Now look again at the passage just quoted from the *Persae.* It proceeds :

Aesch. *Pers.* 92–3

ἀπρόσοιστος γὰρ ὁ Περσῶν στρατὸς ἀλκίφρων τε λαός.

The first of these two figures is plain Ionic a minore. The second is a variation : it contains the same number of longs and shorts, but the third and fourth are inverted : ∪ ∪ ‒ ∪ ‒ ∪ ‒ ‒

instead of ‿‿⏤‿ ‿‿⏤‿. This process of inversion is called *anaclasis*. It is very common in blank verse:

To bé / or nót / to bé: / *thát is* / the quéstion.
Whéther / 'tis nóbler . . .

There, it is the stress-accent that is inverted ; here, the syllabic quantity. And here, the result of the process is the very common rhythm known as Anacreontic, after the poet who invented it :

Anacr. 62

φέρ' ὕδωρ, φέρ' οἶνον, ὦ παῖ,
φέρε δ' ἀνθεμεῦντας ἡμῖν
στεφάνους, ἔνεικον, ὡς δὴ
πρὸς Ἔρωτα πυκταλίζω.

Choriambic too yields a variant by the same process. Instead of ⏤‿‿⏤ ⏤‿‿⏤ we get ⊙⏤‿⏤ ⏤‿‿⏤. This phrase labours, for want of a better, under the name of iambo-choriambic :

Soph. *Trach.* 116–18[1]

οὕτω δὲ τὸν Καδμογενῆ
στρέφει, τὸ δ' αὔξει βιότου
πολύπονον, ὥσπερ πέλαγος. . .

We saw that Dorian rhythm was made up of two figures— **AEOLIAN** one dactylic and the other trochaic. In our third class, which I will call Aeolian[2], these two feet again predominate, but they are more closely combined. Each phrase contains one dactyl and one or more trochees. The most important will be found in Horace :

Hor. *Od.* i 3, 1

Sic te diva potens Cypri.

This is the Glyconic : ⏤⊙ ⏤‿‿ ⏤‿ ⏤ a trochee or spondee, a dactyl, another trochee, and a final long syllable.

---

[1] In the last of these phrases the initial iambus is resolved into three shorts (a tribrach).

[2] I would have called it by its old-fashioned name of logaoedic, but that is now forbidden: see J. M. Edmonds, *Lyra Graeca*, III, p. 617 *n.*

Anacr. 1 1–3

γουνοῦμαί σ᾿, ἐλαφηβόλε,
ξανθὴ παῖ Διός, ἀγρίων
δέσποιν᾿ Ἄρτεμι θηρῶν.

This passage, which begins with two Glyconics, introduces us to another very important Aeolian phrase—the Pherecratic. Its basis is one trochee or spondee, one dactyl, and one spondee: ⏓ – ⏑ ⏑ – –. In both phrases, the dactyl normally occupies second place, but its position varies. In the Pherecratic, it is sometimes the first foot ; in the Glyconic, the first or third :

Soph. *Trach.* 119–21

Κρήσιον· ἀλλά τις θεῶν αἰὲν ἀναμπλάκητον Ἄϊδα σφε δόμων
<u>Glyconic</u>   <u>Glyconic</u>   <u>Pherecratic...</u>
ἐρύκει.

Lastly, we may mention a shorter phrase often found in combination with these two—the Aeolian tripody: – ⏑ ⏑ – ⏑ – or – ⏑ – ⏑ ⏑ – :

Soph. *El.* 245

<u>εἰ γὰρ ὁ μὲν θανὼν</u> γᾶ τε καὶ οὐδὲν ὢν . . .

We have already observed how Ionian rhythm yielded Anacreontic and iambo-choriambic by the process called anaclasis. Aeolian rhythm is varied in the same way. Instead of the normal Glyconic we often find an anaclastic form : ⏑ – – ⏑ ⏑ – ⏑ – for – ⏑ – ⏑ ⏑ – ⏑ –.

Anacr. 6

Μεὶς μὲν δὴ Ποσιδηϊὼν
ἔστηκεν, νεφέλας δ᾿ ὕδωρ
βαρύνει, Δία τ᾿ ἄγριοι
   χειμῶνες κατάγουσιν.

So with the Pherecratic ; instead of the normal – ⏑ – ⏑ ⏑ – – we find ⏑ – – ⏑ ⏑ – – :

Soph. *Phil.* 1123–5

οἴμοι μοι, καί που πολιᾶς
πόντου θινὸς ἐφήμενος,
γελᾷ μου, χερὶ πάλλων.

'Υμὴν ὦ 'Υμέναι' 'Υμήν,
'Υμὴν ὦ 'Υμέναι' ὤ.

Cat. xxxiv 1–4

Dianae sumus in fide
puellae, et pueri integri:
Dianam pueri integri
puellaeque canamus.

Our fourth and last class of rhythm is Paeonic. The im- PAEONIC
portant feet to remember are the cretic ($\overset{\perp}{} \smile \overset{\perp}{}$) and the
bacchius ($\smile \overset{\perp}{} -$):

Aesch. *Supp.* 423–5

φρόντισον καὶ γενοῦ πανδίκως εὐσεβὴς πρόξενος.

Aesch. *Eum.* 791–3

στενάζω; τί ῥέξω; γένωμαι δυσοίστα πολίταις;

The other feet belonging to this class are merely resolved
forms of these two. Thus the cretic may be resolved into the
first paeon ($\overset{\perp}{} \smile \overset{\smile}{\smile}$):

Ar. *Ach.* 216

σπονδοφόρος οὗτος ὑπ' ἐμοῦ τότε διωκόμενος . . .

Similarly, both cretic and bacchius may be resolved into the
fourth paeon ($\overset{\smile}{\smile} \smile \overset{\perp}{}$ or $\smile \overset{\smile}{\smile} -$):

Aesch. *Eum.* 329–30

ἐπὶ δὲ τῷ τεθυμένῳ τόδε μέλος, παρακοπά . . .

Combine any of these feet with an iambus and you get the
Paeonic figure known as the dochmiac. It has many forms,
of which the commonest are: $\smile \overset{\perp}{} - \smile \overset{\perp}{}$ or $\smile \overset{\perp}{} \smile \overset{\perp}{} -$ ("slow"

dochmiac), ⏑⏑⏑⏓⏑⏓ or ⏑⏓⏑⏑⏑⏓[1] ("quick" dochmiac). Most dochmiac passages contain an admixture of cretics and bacchii and often of pure iambic:

Aesch. *Agam.* 249–58

κρόκου βαφὰς δ᾽ ἐς πέδον χέουσα
ἔβαλλ᾽ ἕκαστον θυτήρων ἀπ᾽ ὄμματος βέλει φιλοίκτῳ
πρέπουσά θ᾽ ὡς ἐν γραφαῖς, προσεννέπειν
θέλουσ᾽, ἐπεὶ πολλάκις
πατρὸς κατ᾽ ἀνδρῶνας εὐτραπέζους
ἔμελψεν. ἀγνᾷ δ᾽ ἀταύρωτος αὐδᾷ
πατρὸς φίλου τριτόσπονδον εὔποτμον παιᾶνα φίλως ἐτίμα.
                                                              Pherecratic

Instead of ⏑⏑⏑⏓ ⏑⏓ we sometimes find ⏓⏑⏑⏓ ⏑⏓; that is to say, the initial syllable of this form of the dochmiac is sometimes long:

Aesch. *P. V.* 618–19

πόθεν ἐμοῦ σὺ πατρὸς ὄνομ᾽ ἀπύεις;
εἰπέ μοι τᾷ μογερᾷ τίς ὤν . . .

This completes our examination of the more common standard phrases. In the course of our enquiry we shall come across others which will be readily recognised as variants based on these types. Let us now consider how these phrases are combined in groups so as to form the rhythmical period or sentence.

---

[1] There is also another form found in dochmiac, which is sufficiently common to deserve mention here : ⏑⏓ – ⏓. Cf. Aesch. *Agam.* 379 Διὸς πλαγάν.

CHAPTER THREE

THE SENTENCE

TURNING back for a moment to the Irish air quoted at the head of the last chapter, we remember that the phrase, and not the bar or the figure, was the smallest unit which could convey to the ear an adequate impression of the rhythm. But even the phrase is not entirely self-contained. We feel that, although the first of the two phrases comes to an end in the middle of the fourth bar, the rhythm continues without a break to the climax in the eighth. In other words, the two phrases must be taken together as parts of a single musical *sentence*. The first phrase, as it were, raises our expectations; the second satisfies them. The first makes an announcement; the second answers it with an appropriate responsion.

The stanza of modern verse is built up in the same way. Read, for example, the opening of Drayton's *Agincourt*:

> Fair stood the wind for France—

that is the announcing phrase. It is twice repeated:

> When we our sails advance,
> Nor now to prove our chance—

we feel that the rhythm is moving towards a climax. And so it is:

> Fair stood the wind for France,
> When we our sails advance,
> Nor now to prove our chance
> Longer will tarry.

The ear is satisfied; the stanza is complete. The last verse has rounded off the rhythmical period with a suitable *cadence*. Or read the well-known Aeolian couplet:

> ῾Τμὴν ὦ ῾Τμέναι᾿ ῾Τμήν,
> ῾Τμὴν ὦ ῾Τμέναι᾿ ὦ.

That, too, is a complete sentence. The Glyconic announces, the Pherecratic responds. Reverse the order of the two phrases, and this sense of completeness is lost. The Pherecratic is a natural cadence, the Glyconic is not. Different rhythms demand different cadences. A favourite one in Dorian rhythm is a phrase of pure epitrite:

Pind. *O.* vi 19–21

οὔτε δύσηρις ἐὼν οὔτ' ὢν φιλόνικος ἄγαν,
καὶ μέγαν ὅρκον ὀμόσσαις τοῦτό γέ οἱ σαφέως
μαρτυρήσω· μελίφθογγοι δ' ἐπιτρέψοντι Μοῖσαι.

Ionic a minore finds its most complete cadence in its anaclastic form, the Anacreontic. Another, less complete, is obtained by the same process in a different way. Just as choriambic (– ᴗ ᴗ –) gives two iambi (ᴗ – ᴗ –), so Ionic a minore gives two trochees (– ᴗ – ᴗ):

Aesch. *Supp.* 1029–36[1]

ἴτε μὰν ἄστυδ' ἄνακτας μάκαρας θεοὺς γανάεντες πολιούχους
τε καὶ οἳ χεῦμ' Ἐρασίνου περιναίουσιν παλαιόν.
ὑποδέξασθε δ' ὀπαδοὶ μέλος· αἶνος δὲ πόλιν τήνδε Πελασγῶν
ἐχέτω, μηδ' ἔτι Νείλου προχοὰς σέβωμεν ὕμνοις.

Choriambic tends to slip into Aeolian:

Soph. *Phil.* 714–15

οἰνοχύτου πώματος ἤσθη δεκέτη χρόνον.
Aeol. tripody

In Aeolian rhythm the usual cadence is Pherecratic, of which an example has just been given. The same phrase is often used as a cadence in Paeonic. An example will be found at the end of the dochmiac passage from the *Agamemnon* which was quoted in the last chapter[2].

---

[1] 1029 ἄστυδ' ἄνακτας Tucker: ἀστυάνακτας. 1031 περιναίουσιν Marckscheffel: περιναίετε.   [2] See above, p. 12.

The announcement does not necessarily consist of only a single phrase. A favourite device is to follow up one sentence with another, which repeats the general scheme of the first, but with a longer announcement:

Anacr. 1

γουνοῦμαί σ', ἐλαφηβόλε,   (First sentence)
ξανθὴ παῖ Διός, ἀγρίων
δέσποιν' Ἄρτεμι θηρῶν·
ἥ κου νῦν ἐπὶ Ληθαίου   (Second sentence)
δίνῃσι θρασυκαρδίων
ἀνδρῶν ἐσκατορᾷς πόλιν
χαίρουσ'· οὐ γὰρ ἀνημέρους
ποιμαίνεις πολιήτας.

This device will be familiar to Englishmen:

God save our gracious King,   (First sentence)
Long live our noble King,
God save the King.
Send him victorious,   (Second sentence)
Happy and glorious,
Long to reign over us;
God save the King.

Nor are all the announcing phrases necessarily identical. The following sentence begins with an Ionian phrase (‒⌣ ⌣⌣‒ ⌣‒)[1] and a Glyconic:

Soph. *O.T.* 1186–8

ἰὼ γενεαὶ βροτῶν, ὡς ὑμᾶς ἴσα καὶ τὸ μηδὲν ζώσας ἐναριθμῶ.

This scheme is repeated in the sentence which follows, except that there we have two Glyconics instead of one:

Ibid. 1189–92

τίς γάρ, τίς ἀνὴρ πλέον τᾶς εὐδαιμονίας φέρει
ἢ τοσοῦτον ὅσον δοκεῖν καὶ δόξαντ' ἀποκλῖναι;

[1] For this and other Ionian phrases, see Appendix

PRO-
TRACTION

The final cadence may be strengthened by extending it
beyond its normal length:

Soph. *Trach.* 947–9

πότερα πρότερον ἐπιστένω, πότερα τέλεα περαιτέρω,
<u>Glyconic (resolved)</u>   Repeat
δύσκριτ' ἔμοιγε δυστάνῳ.
Pherecratic (protracted)

The last of these three phrases is a Pherecratic augmented to
the extent of one syllable: ⏔⏑⏑⏔⏑⏔–– instead of ⏔⏑⏑⏔⏑⏔–.
The effect is heavy, and appropriate to the sense. The same
device is used in Dorian rhythm, where the epitrite may be
protracted in this way:

Stesich. 32

οὐκ ἔστ' ἔτυμος λόγος οὗτος·
οὐδ' ἔβας ἐν ναυσὶν εὐσέλμοις.
Epitrite (protracted)

Nor is it confined to the end of the sentence: wherever
the poetical effect is slow, heavy or laboured, we may expect
it to be enforced by protraction. Perhaps the finest example
is found in the *Eumenides*, where the Furies, rising out of
sleep, begin their binding-song with an invocation of their
dread mother, Night:

Aesch. *Eum.* 322–4

μᾶτερ, ἅ μ' ἔτικτες, ὦ μᾶτερ Νύξ,
ἀλαοῖσι καὶ δεδορκόσιν ποινάν,....

OVERLAP

A still more effective means of enforcing the final cadence
is provided by another musical device known as *overlap*. Let
us continue our analysis of that strophe from the *Oedipus
Tyrannus* (1186–96): ἰὼ γενεαὶ βροτῶν. We have seen that
the second sentence is a repetition of the first, except that
the Pherecratic cadence is held up, and so enforced, by the
interposition of an additional Glyconic. Our third sentence

is to bring the strophe to an end, and so will require a cadence even more forcible than either of the preceding:

Soph. *O.T.* 1193–6

τὸν σόν τοι παράδειγμ᾽ ἔχων, τὸν σὸν δαίμονα, τὸν σόν, ὦ
Glyconic   Glyconic
                   Pherecratic
τλᾶμον Οἰδιπόδα, βροτῶν οὐδὲν μακαρίζω.
Glyconic

The announcement consists, as before, of a Glyconic twice repeated; the cadence, as before, of a Pherecratic. But here the Pherecratic is dovetailed into the preceding Glyconic in such a way that, if the rhythmical effect is to be fully appreciated, the second syllable of βροτῶν must be regarded as common to both. This is very important.

Ar. *Ach.* 836–41

εὐδαιμονεῖ γ᾽ ἄνθρωπος· οὐκ ἤκουσας οἳ προβαίνει
1   2
τὸ πρᾶγμα τοῦ βουλεύματος; καρπώσεται γὰρ ἀνὴρ
1   2
ἐν τἀγορᾷ καθήμενος· κἂν εἰσίῃ τις Κτησίας
1   1
                Pherecratic
ἢ συκοφάντης ἄλλος, οἰμώζων καθεδεῖται.
1

Aesch. *Eum.* 329–31
                           Pherecratic
ἐπὶ δὲ τῷ τεθυμένῳ τόδε μέλος, παρακοπά, παραφορὰ φρενοδαλής
Fourth paeons

We are now in a better position to understand that Choriambic-Aeolian rhythm noticed above:

Soph. *Phil.* 714–15
Choriambic
οἰνοχύτου πώματος ἥσθη δεκέτη χρόνον
              Aeolian tripody

T   2

Aesch. *Supp.* 553–5

Choriambic

$$\overline{\text{ἀντίπορον γαῖαν ἐν αἴσᾳ διατέμνουσα πόρον κυματίαν ὁρίζει.}}$$
                                                                    Pherecratic
So in English:

$$\overline{\text{None but the brave, none but the brave, none but the brave deserves}}$$
    the fair.

You would spoil that rhythm if you read it thus:

None but the brave, none but the brave, none but the brave
Deserves the fair.

THE
SAPPHIC
STANZA

Unfortunately, many Greek rhythms are spoiled, or at least obscured, by the way in which they are printed. Take the Sapphic stanza[1]:

Sappho 2

φαίνεταί μοι κῆνος ἴσος θέοισιν
ἔμμεν ὤνηρ ὅστις ἐναντίος τοι
ἰζάνει καὶ πλασίον ἆδυ φωνεύσας ὑπακούει.

Is that the right way to read it? Does not the ear feel instinctively that the third and fourth lines should be taken more closely together?

φαίνεταί μοι κῆνος ἴσος θέοισιν
ἔμμεν ὤνηρ ὅστις ἐναντίος τοι
ἰζάνει καὶ πλασίον ἆδυ φωνεύσας ὑπακούει.

That is how anyone with an ear for rhythm reads the stanza, and that is how it ought to be printed. If we hesitate to accept the authority of our ears, we have only to notice that hiatus is not allowed between the third and fourth lines, as usually printed, though between the others it is common, and

---

[1] This account of the Sapphic stanza is taken from W. Headlam, *Illustrations of Greek Metre*, ii (Camb. Univ. Press). See also Lobel, *Sappho*, p. lxvi.

that a single word is often divided between the third and fourth, between the others never[1]. How, then, is the stanza to be analysed?

$$\underset{\text{Epitrite} \quad \text{Pherecratic}}{\underline{\phi\alpha\acute{\iota}\nu\epsilon\tau\alpha\acute{\iota} \ \mu o\iota \ \kappa\hat{\eta}\nu o\varsigma \ \acute{\iota}\sigma o\varsigma \ \theta\acute{\epsilon}o\iota\sigma\iota\nu}}$$

That is clear enough. The first phrase is made up of two figures—an epitrite and a Pherecratic. Sappho is mixing her rhythms. And the second is a repetition of the first:

$$\ \acute{\epsilon}\mu\mu\epsilon\nu \ \acute{\omega}\nu\eta\rho \ \acute{o}\sigma\tau\iota\varsigma \ \acute{\epsilon}\nu\alpha\nu\tau\acute{\iota}o\varsigma \ \tau o\iota$$

So is the third—but with a difference. Being the last of the stanza, it ends with a more perfect cadence than either of the preceding:

Epitrite Pherecratic
$$\underline{\overline{\ }\ }$$
$$\underset{\text{Pherecratic}}{\underline{\iota\zeta\acute{\alpha}\nu\epsilon\iota \ \kappa\alpha\grave{\iota} \ \pi\lambda\alpha\sigma\acute{\iota}o\nu \ \acute{\alpha}\delta\upsilon \ \phi\omega\nu\epsilon\acute{\upsilon}\sigma\alpha\varsigma \ \acute{\upsilon}\pi\alpha\kappa o\acute{\upsilon}\epsilon\iota.}}$$

Is not this very beautiful?

---

[1] Horace remodelled the Sapphic, as he remodelled other Greek lyric metres: he allows hiatus, and does not usually run his words over. But sometimes he wrote in the Greek style: cf. *Carm.* I. ii. 19, xxv. 11, also Catull. xi. 9–12, 17–20.

CHAPTER FOUR

METHODS OF TRANSITION

THE sentences we examined in the last chapter were mostly homogeneous; that is to say, their component phrases were all drawn from one or other of the four recognised classes of rhythm. But the Greek poet did not hesitate to mix his rhythms, when the effect seemed to require it, and indeed we find every variety of sentence, from complete homogeneity to the utmost diversity. Some phrases have natural affinities with each other, irrespective of the class to which they belong, and these may be freely mixed without violence to the ear. Such are the Aeolian tripody and the dochmiac, happily combined by Aeschylus in *The Suppliants*:

Aesch. *Supp.* 641–6[1]

μήποτε πυρίφατον	τάνδε Πελασγίαν	τὸν ἄχορον βοὰν
Aeolian tripody	Aeolian tripody	Dochmiac

κτίσαι μάχλον Ἄρη,	τὸν ἀρότοις θερίζοντα βροτοὺς	ἐν ἄλλοις.
Dochmiac	Dochmiac	Pherecratic

Others, however, do not possess this natural affinity. If they are to be satisfactorily combined, the poet must find some means of mitigating the abruptness of the transition. There are five such methods of transition, or shifts as they may be called: shift by anacrusis, resolution, link, echo and overlap[2].

I. ANACRUSIS.

If we look back at the phrases we have been considering in the preceding chapters, we shall find that they may be divided into two classes according to the disposition of the

---

[1] 642 τάνδε Πελασγίαν Klausen: τὰν Πελασγίαν πόλιν.

[2] See Headlam, *J.H.S.* vol. XXII, pp. 216–19, for shift by echo, link and overlap.

rhythmical accents. First, there are the phrases based on such feet as the iambus and anapaest, which begin with an unaccented syllable. These are in what is called *rising* rhythm. And secondly, there are the phrases based on such feet as the trochee and dactyl, which begin with an accented syllable. These are in *falling* rhythm. There is a peculiar feature of falling rhythm which must now be explained; though it is so common in the poetry of all languages that it hardly needs explanation.

> With a waist and with a side
> White as Hebe's, when her zone
> Slipt its golden clasp, and down
> Fell her kirtle to her feet,
> While she held the goblet sweet,
> And Jove grew languid.—Break the mesh
> Of the Fancy's silken leash ;
> Quickly break her prison-string,
> And such joys as these she'll bring.

This passage is plainly in falling rhythm. The feet correspond to the Greek trochee, and begin with the rhythmical accent—all except the last line but three : "And Jove grew languid...." What are we to make of it? If it stood alone, we might take it as rising rhythm (iambi): "And Jove / grew lang/uid,—Break / the leash." But the context compels us to take it in falling rhythm like the rest :

> Fell her / kirtle / to her / feet,
> While she / held the / goblet / sweet,
> And / Jove grew / languid....

The initial syllable stands outside the metrical scheme. This is anacrusis. In Greek, too, falling rhythm is frequently varied by the addition of a prefix of this kind—usually a single syllable, long or short, more rarely two shorts.

Stesich. 32

οὐκ ἔστ' ἔτυμος λόγος οὗτος
Prosodiac with anacrusis

Alcm. 23. 36–7

ἔστι τις σιῶν τισις.   ὁ δ' ὄλβιος ὅστις εὔφρων . . .

<u>Trochaic</u>   <u>Pherecratic with anacrusis</u>

Pind. *P.* iii 23

<u>μεταμώνια θηρεύων</u> ἀκράντοις ἐλπίσιν.

Prosodiac with anacr.

It is not difficult to see how anacrusis comes to be used as a means of transition between rising and falling rhythm:

Aesch. *Supp.* 800–5[1]

πόθεν δέ μοι γένοιτ' ἂν αἰθέρος θρόνος,
πρὸς ὃν χιὼν ὑδρηλὰ γίγνεται νέφη,
ἢ λισσὰς αἰγίλιψ ἀπρόσδερκτος οἰόφρων κρεμὰς
γυπιὰς πέτρα, βαθὺ πτῶμα μαρτυροῦσά μοι . . .

After two iambic trimeters we hear the phrase ‒⏌ ⏌⏌ ⏌⏌ ⏌⏌, an iambic dimeter, which, while continuing the rising rhythm with which we began, at the same time suggests trochaic with anacrusis, and so provides an easy transition to the trochaic phrases which follow.

Soph. *Ant.* 948–55

<u>καίτοι καὶ γενεᾷ τίμιος</u>, ὦ παῖ παῖ,

<u>καὶ Ζηνὸς ταμιεύεσκε</u> γονὰς χρυσορύτους·

<u>ἀλλ' ἁ μοιριδία τις</u> δύνασις δεινά·

These are prosodiacs—strongly marked falling rhythm. Hence, when we come to the next two phrases—

οὔτ' ἄν νιν ὄλβος οὔτ' Ἄρης,
οὐ πύργος, οὐχ ἁλίκτυποι

we take them as also in falling rhythm—trochaic with anacrusis. But trochaic with anacrusis suggests iambic, rising, rhythm, and by this means we are enabled to pass to dochmiac:

<u>κελαιναὶ νᾶες</u> ἐκφύγοιεν.

---

[1] 801 χιὼν...νέφη Porson: νέφη δ'...χιών. 802–3 ἀπρόσδερκτος Weil: ἀπρόσδεικτος.

Soph. *Ant.* 332-8

<u>πολλὰ τὰ δεινὰ κοὐδὲν ἀνθρώπου δεινότερον πέλει·</u>
<u>τοῦτο καὶ πολιοῦ πέραν πόντου χειμερίῳ νότῳ</u>
<u>χωρεῖ, περῖβρυχίοισιν . . .</u>
Pherecratic with anacrusis

This is an Aeolian sentence of a type with which we are already familiar. But the closing Pherecratic has anacrusis. And so we proceed in rising rhythm:

περῶν ὑπ᾽ οἴδμασιν, θεῶν τε τὰν ὑπερτάταν, Γᾶν . . .

II. RESOLUTION.

There is another, more subtle, means of transition between rising and falling rhythm. An iambus may be resolved into a tribrach (◡ ⏌ into ◡ ◟◡): so may a trochee (⏌ ◡ into ◟◡ ◡). Hence the tribrach provides a convenient link between the two.

Aesch. *Cho.* 22-5[1]

<u>ἰαλτὸς ἐκ δόμων ἔβην χοὰς προπομπὸς ὀξύχειρι συν κόπῳ.</u>
Iambic dimeter   Iambic trimeter
<u>πρέπει παρῇσι φοινίαις ἀμυγμὸς ὄνυχος ἄλοκι νεοτόμῳ.</u>

The first three phrases are iambic. The fourth opens with three tribrachs, which might be iambic too. Only when we reach the end of the phrase do we realise that they stand for trochaic: ◟◡ ◡ ◟◡ ◡ ◟◡ ◡ ⏌.

Aesch. *P. V.* 169-76

<u>τίς ὧδε τλησικάρδιος θεῶν ὅτῳ τάδ᾽ ἐπιχαρῆ;</u>
Iambic   Iambic
<u>τίς οὐ ξυνασχαλᾷ κακοῖς τεοῖσι, δίχα γε Διός; ὁ δ᾽ ἐπικότως ἀεὶ</u>
Iambic   Iambic
<u>θέμενος ἄγναμπτον νόον δάμναται Οὐρανίαν γένναν, οὐδὲ λήξει.</u>
Epitr. resolved   Epitrite   Prosodiac   Epitrite

The first four phrases are iambic (rising rhythm). In the fifth, we pass to Dorian (falling rhythm): but the transition is made

---

[1] 24 παρῇσι Hermann: παρηὶς. φοινίαις ἀμυγμός Conington: φοινισσ᾽ ἀμυγμοῖς.

easy by the resolution of the first foot of the epitrite : ◡◡◡ ⏑–
instead of ⏑◡ ⏑–.

Soph. *Aj.* 605–7

χρόνῳ τρυχόμενος, κακὰν ἐλπίδ' ἔχων
<u>rising</u>   <u>rising</u>

ἔτι μέ ποτ' ἀνύσειν τὸν ἀπότροπον ἀΐδηλον Ἀΐδαν.
<u>shift to falling</u>   <u>Aeolian enneasyllable (resolved)[1]</u>

A pretty example of shift by resolution is to be found in Pindar's first Olympian—a composition we will examine in detail in a later chapter :

Pind. *O.* i 7–8

Trochaic
μηδ' Ὀλυμπίας ἀγῶνα φέρτερον αὐδάσομεν·
<u>Pherecratic</u>
ὅθεν ὁ πολύφατος ὕμνος ἀμφιβάλλεται . . .

The first of these two phrases is in falling rhythm, though a hint of rising is contained in the iambus appended at the end. The second begins with two tribrachs. Of these the first, ὅθεν/ὁ, is so divided as to suggest trochaic, while the second, πολύφα, is doubtful, and so prepares the way for the undisguised iambic which follows, and for the rising rhythm which continues to the end of the strophe.

III. LINK.

Some figures and phrases contain in themselves the elements of both rising and falling rhythm. The fourth paeon, for example, may stand for a cretic, which is in falling rhythm (◡◡◡⏑ for ⏑◡⏑), or for a bacchius (◡◡◡⏑ for ◡⏑–), in which

---

[1] See Appendix. Thus the last phrase of the strophe echoes the first (596–7): ὦ κλεινὰ Σάλαμις, σὺ μέν που. Cf. *Phil.* 827 "Ὕπν' ὀδύνας ἀδαής, "Ὕπνε δ' ἀλγέων = 838 πολύ τι πολὺ παρὰ πόδα κράτος ἄρνυται. Resolution is used, not as a shift, but as an anticipation of a change of rhythm, in Soph. *Trach.* 116–19 (see above, pp. 9–10), where πολύπονον (for ◡⏑◡) anticipates the dactyl Κρήσιον : cf. Aesch. *Theb.* 818 γένεος. For other cases of shift by resolution, cf. Eur. *H. F.* 413 ἄγορον, *El.* 480 ἔκανεν, *Hel.* 341 πότερα.

case it is in rising rhythm. Hence it comes to be used as a shift from one to the other.

Aesch. *Supp.* 787–91[1]

μέλας γενοίμαν καπνὸς νέφεσσι γειτονῶν Διός,
Iambic (rising)   Iambic (rising)
τὸ πᾶν δ' ἄφαντος ἀμπετὴς ἄϊστος ὡς
Iambic (rising)
κόνις ἄτερθε πτερύγων ὀλοίμαν.
Paeon (link) Pherecratic (falling)

In the same way, the so-called iambo-choriambic ($\cup \perp \cup \perp$ $\perp \cup \cup \perp$) may be regarded as beginning in rising (iambic), and as ending in falling (choriambic) rhythm. That is why it is used in the following passage:

Aesch. *Cho.* 48–52

ἰὼ πάνοιζυς ἑστία, ἰὼ κατασκαφαὶ δόμων ἀνήλιοι, βροτοστυγεῖς
Iambic (rising)   Iambic (rising)   Iambic (rising)
δνόφοι καλύπτουσι δόμους δεσποτῶν θανάτοισι.
Iambo-choriambic (link)   Pherecratic (falling)

The transition is sometimes effected by a non-descript phrase invented for the occasion:

Aesch. *Agam.* 745–8

δύσεδρος καὶ δυσόμιλος συμένα Πρῑαμίδαισιν,
Ionic a minore (rising)
πομπᾷ Διὸς ξενίου, νυμφόκλαυτος Ἐρινύς.
Link   Pherecratic (falling)

Aesch. *Supp.* 879–82

καὶ γὰρ δυσπαλάμως ὄλοιο
Aeolian enneasyllable
δι' ἁλίρρυτον ἄλσος κατὰ Σαρπηδόνιον χῶμα πολύψαμμον
Link   Ionic a minore
    ἀλαθείς.

---

[1] 790 ἀμπετὴς ἄϊστος ὡς Haupt: ἀμπετήσαισ δόσωσ.

IV. Echo.

The dominant factor in the rhythm of Greek lyric, as was suggested at the outset of this inquiry, is the natural rhythm dictated by the sense of the words. Sometimes, especially in the case of the simpler and commoner rhythms, the words are so grouped as to break across the outlines of the metrical pattern, thus creating a rhythmical undercurrent, as it were, of their own. Common dochmiac, for example, can be so arranged as to suggest trochaic :

Aesch. *Agam.* 202–3

Dochmiac	Dochmiac

πνοαὶ δ' ἀπὸ Στρυμόνος μολοῦσαι
(Trochaic)

Dochmiac	Dochmiac

κακόσχολοι, νήστιδες, δύσορμοι . . .
(Trochaic)

Often the purpose of such effects is merely to give the ear variety; but the poet is quick to take advantage of them for another purpose:

Aesch. *Agam.* 387–91[1]

Dochmiac	Dochmiac	Dochmiac	Dochmiac

πνεόντων μεῖζον ἢ δικαίως, φλεόντων δωμάτων ὑπέρφευ
(Trochaic)　　　　　　　　　(Trochaic)

Dochmiac	Dochmiac	Trochaic (echo)

ὑπὲρ τὸ βέλτιστον. ἔστω δ' ἀπήμαντον ὥστ' ἀπαρκεῖν

Pherecratic

εὖ πραπίδων λαχόντι.

The trochaic movement is at first heard as an undercurrent running beneath the rising rhythm of the dochmiacs; but presently it emerges as an independent phrase, and so affords an easy transition to the falling rhythm of the final Pherecratic.

---

[1] 391 λαχόντι Headlam : λαχόντα.

Aesch. *Supp.* 58–63[1]

εἰ δὲ κυρεῖ τις πέλας οἰωνοπολῶν ἔγγαιος οἶκτον ἀΐων,

Choriambic	Trochaic with anacrusis

δοξάσει τις ἀκούειν

Pherecratic

ὄπα τᾶς Τηρείας μήτιδος οἰκτρᾶς ἀλόχου κιρκηλάτου τ᾽ ἀηδόνος.

Ionic a minore	Trochaic

The latter part of the Pherecratic (τις ἀκούειν) suggests Ionic a minore : and this is echoed at the beginning of the next phrase (ὄπα τᾶς Τη-), which continues in Ionic a minore.

Aesch. *Theb.* 712–3[2]

Ionic a minore	Aeolian decasyllable[3]

κατάρας Οἰδιπόδα βλαψίφρονος· παιδολέτωρ δ᾽ Ἔρις ἐξοτρύνει.

echo

Soph. *O. C.* 121–37

Molottus (᷉−᷉) and cretic	Molottus and cretic

προσδέρκου, λεῦσσέ νιν, προσπεύθου πανταχῇ.

Bacchius	Anaclastic Glyconic

πλανάτας, πλανάτας τις ὁ πρέσβυς, οὐδ᾽

echo

Glyconic

ἔγχωρος· προσέβα γὰρ οὐκ

Glyconic	Glyconic

ἄν ποτ᾽ ἀστιβὲς ἄλσος ἐς τᾶνδ᾽ ἀμαιμακετᾶν κορᾶν,

Aeolian tripody	Aeolian tripody

ἃς τρέμομεν λέγειν, καὶ παραμειβόμεσθ᾽

Bacchius	Anaclastic Glyconic	Glyconic

ἀδέρκτως, ἀφώνως, ἀλόγως τὸ τᾶς εὐφάμου στόμα φροντίδος

echo

Anaclastic Glyconic	Pherecratic

ἱέντες· τὰ δὲ νῦν τιν᾽ ἥκειν λόγος οὐδὲν ἄζονθ᾽

echo

---

[1] 58 οἰωνοπολῶν Headlam, after Tucker: οἰωνοπόλων. 59 οἶκτον Schwenk : οἶκτον οἰκτρὸν.

[2] 713 ἐξοτρύνει Headlam : ἄδ᾽ ὀτρύνει.

[3] See Appendix for this phrase. Its function here is to combine an echo of choriambic with the Pherecratic cadence.

Anapaests

ὃν ἐγὼ λεύσσων περὶ πᾶν οὔπω δύναμαι τέμενος

γνῶναι ποῦ μοί ποτε ναίει.

In this last passage—an excellent example of the uses of the echo—the cretic πανταχῇ is followed by a bacchius (πλανάτας), which is repeated as the opening of an anaclastic Glyconic¹, and so prepares us for common Glyconic. We hear the bacchius again at ἀδέρκτως: again it is taken up as the opening of an anaclastic Glyconic, and so we come back to common Glyconic again. The bacchius is re-echoed a third time in ἱέντες, thus preparing the ear for the rising rhythm of the anapaests, which bring this beautiful strophe to an end.

Sophocles, of all the poets, delighted in the effects which can be obtained from this device of echo. In his pursuit of them, he sometimes abandons the standard phrase almost entirely, and gives free rein to his fancy, allowing one rhythm to grow out of another, phrase upon phrase, just as they suggest themselves to his sensitive ear. Thus, the following passage is based on certain standard phrases (given above the words): but it owes its organic unity to the delicate interplay of echoes (given below the words).

Soph. *Aj.* 221–32²

Epitrite³	Epitrite	Prosodiac	Epitrite
οἵαν ἐδήλωσας ἀνδρὸς		αἴθονος ἀγγελίαν	ἄτλατον οὐδὲ φευκτάν,
a		b	c

Prosodiac		Prosodiacs	
τῶν μεγάλων Δαναῶν ὕπο κληζομέναν,		τὰν ὁ μέγας μῦθος ἀέξει.	
b echoed	d	d echoed	e

¹ Cf. Eur. *Supp.* 1012–13 ὁρῶ δὴ τελευτὰν ἵν᾽ ἔστακα· τύχα δέ μοι.

² See Headlam, *J.H.S.* vol. XXII, pp. 218–9.

³ _⏑_⏑ for ⏑⏑_⏑⏑_: see Appendix.

Iambo-choriambic	Pherecratic

οἴμοι φοβοῦμαι τὸ προσέρπον. περίφαντος ἀνὴρ
a echoed   e echoed   f

g

Anaclastic Pherecratic

θανεῖται, παραπλάκτῳ χερὶ συγκατακτὰς
f echoed   e echoed   g echoed

Prosodiac	Epitrite

κελαινοῖς ξίφεσιν βοτὰ καὶ βοτῆρας ἱππονώμας.
f echoed   c echoed

V. OVERLAP.

The use of overlap for enforcing the final cadence has
already been illustrated. As a shift, it is not confined to the
cadence.

Soph. *El.* 1064–9

Aeolian couplet[1]

καὶ τὰν Οὐρανίαν Θέμιν δαρὸν οὐκ ἀπόνητοι.

Glyconic

ὦ χθονία βροτοῖσι Φάμα, κατά μοι βόασον οἰκτρὰν	
Anacreontic	Anacreontic

ὄπα τοῖς ἔνερθ᾽ Ἀτρείδαις ἀχόρευτα φέρουσ᾽ ὀνείδη.	
Anacreontic	Pherecratic with anacrusis

Eur. *Hel.* 1451–5

Iambo-choriambic	Iambo-choriambic

Φοίνισσα Σιδωνιὰς ὦ ταχεῖα κώπα ῥοθίοισι, μάτηρ
                                      Pherecratic

Glyconic	Pherecratic

εἰρεσίας φίλα, χοραγὲ τῶν καλλιχόρων δελφίνων, ὅταν αὔραις...
                    Iambo-choriambic

Aesch. *P. V.* 412–17[2]

Iambo-choriambic	Iambo-choriambic

στένω σε τᾶς οὐλομένας τύχας, Προμηθεῦ· δακρυσίστακτα δ᾽
              Anacreontic   Ionic a minore . .

---

[1] I give the name Aeolian couplet, for the sake of convenience, to the Glyconic
followed by a Pherecratic.

[2] 415 δακρυσίστακτα Minckwitz: δακρυσίστακτον.

$$\underline{\mathrm{\dot{a}\pi' \; \ddot{o}\sigma\sigma\omega\nu \; \dot{\rho}a\delta\iota\nu\hat{\omega}\nu \; \lambda\epsilon\iota\beta o\mu\acute{\epsilon}\nu a \; \dot{\rho}\acute{\epsilon}os \; \pi a\rho\epsilon\iota\grave{a}\nu}}$$
(*contd.*)　　　　　　　Anacreontic

$$\underline{\nu o\tau\acute{\iota}o\iota s \; \ddot{\epsilon}\tau\epsilon\gamma\xi a \; \pi\eta\gamma a\hat{\iota}s.}$$
Anacreontic

Overlap reaches its highest point of development in a continuous contrapuntal effect, in which two different rhythms are made to run side by side for the duration of several CONCUR- phrases. This may be called *concurrent* rhythm[1].
RENCE

Aesch. *P. V.* 130–40

Iambo-choriambic　　　　Iambo-choriambic
$$\underline{\mu\eta\delta\grave{\epsilon}\nu \; \phi o\beta\eta\theta\hat{\eta}s\cdot} \; \underline{\phi\iota\lambda\acute{\iota}a \; \gamma\grave{a}\rho \; \ddot{\eta}\delta\epsilon \; \tau\acute{a}\xi\iota s} \; \underline{\pi\tau\epsilon\rho\acute{\upsilon}\gamma\omega\nu}$$
　　　　　　Anacreontic　　　　Anacreontic...
Iambo-choriambic
$$\underline{\theta o a\hat{\iota}s \; \dot{a}\mu\acute{\iota}\lambda\lambda a\iota s \; \pi\rho o\sigma\acute{\epsilon}\beta a}$$
(*contd.*)
Pherecratic　　　　　Iambo-choriambic
$$\underline{\tau\acute{o}\nu\delta\epsilon \; \pi\acute{a}\gamma o\nu,} \; \underline{\pi a\tau\rho\acute{\omega}as \; \mu\acute{o}\gamma\iota s \; \pi a\rho\epsilon\acute{\iota}\pi o\upsilon\sigma a \; \phi\rho\acute{\epsilon}\nu as\cdot}$$
Aeolian decasyllable
$$\underline{\kappa\rho a\iota\pi\nu o\phi\acute{o}\rho o\iota \; \delta\acute{\epsilon} \; \mu' \; \ddot{\epsilon}\pi\epsilon\mu\psi a\nu \; a\check{\upsilon}\rho a\iota.}$$
(Pherecratic)
Iambo-choriambic　　　　Iambo-choriambic
$$\underline{\kappa\tau\acute{\upsilon}\pi o\upsilon \; \gamma\grave{a}\rho \; \dot{a}\chi\grave{\omega}} \; \underline{\chi\acute{a}\lambda\upsilon\beta os \; \delta\iota\hat{\eta}\xi\epsilon\nu \; \ddot{a}\nu\tau\rho\omega\nu \; \mu\upsilon\chi\acute{o}\nu, \; \dot{\epsilon}\kappa \; \delta'}$$
　　　　　　Anacreontic　　　　Anacreontic...
Iambo-choriambic
$$\underline{\ddot{\epsilon}\pi\lambda\eta\xi\acute{\epsilon} \; \mu o\upsilon \; \tau\grave{a}\nu \; \theta\epsilon\mu\epsilon\rho\hat{\omega}\pi\iota\nu \; a\grave{\iota}\delta\hat{\omega}\cdot}$$
(*contd.*)　　　Pherecratic
Aeolian decasyllable
$$\underline{\sigma\acute{\upsilon}\theta\eta\nu \; \delta' \; \dot{a}\pi\acute{\epsilon}\delta\iota\lambda os \; \ddot{o}\chi\omega \; \pi\tau\epsilon\rho\omega\tau\hat{\omega}.}$$
(Pherecratic)

The concurrent phrases are iambo-choriambic and Anacreontic. Both are indispensable to the design—the first because it forms the basis of the metrical pattern, the second because the natural grouping of the words demands it. If we analyse the first sentence, for example, as iambo-choriambic alone—

---

[1] See Headlam, *J.H.S.* vol. XXII, pp. 219–21.

μηδὲν φοβηθῆς· φιλία
γὰρ ἥδε τάξις πτερύγων
θοαῖς ἁμίλλαις προσέβα. . .

the result looks well enough on paper, but does not satisfy
the ear; for the dominant rhythm of the middle of the sentence
is Anacreontic:

μηδὲν φοβηθῆς·
φιλία γὰρ ἥδε τάξις
πτερύγων θοαῖς ἁμίλλαις
προσέβα. . .

The distinctive feature of the passage as a whole is its lack of
phrase-pauses. Before we approach the end of one phrase we
are carried onwards by the beginning of the next. The effect
is undulating. Could Aeschylus have devised a happier
rhythmical accompaniment to the flight of his Ocean Nymphs
as they ride through the air on their winged sea-horses?
Perhaps that is why Sophocles uses the same rhythm in a
passage in the *Electra*:

Soph. *El.* 1058–62

Iambo-choriambic	Iambo-choriambic	Iambo-choriambic...

τί τοὺς ἄνωθεν φρονιμωτάτους οἰωνοὺς ἐσορώμενοι τροφᾶς κη-

Anacreontic		Anacreontic

(*contd.*) Iambo-choriambic		Iambo-choriambic...

δομένους ἀφ᾽ ὧν τε βλάστωσιν ἀφ᾽ ὧν τ᾽ ὄνασιν εὕρω-

Anacreontic	Anacreontic

(*contd.*)

σι, τάδ᾽ οὐκ ἐπ᾽ ἴσας τελοῦμεν;

Pherecratic

In the *Ajax*, he compounds Anacreontic in the same way
with Glyconic:

Soph. *Aj.* 695–701

Glyconic	Glyconic

ὦ Πὰν Πὰν ἁλίπλαγκτε Κυλλανίας χιονοκτύπου

Anaclastic Glyconic	Anacreontic...

πετραίας ἀπὸ δειράδος

(*contd.*) Anacreontic...

Glyconic   Glyconic

φάνηθ᾽, ὦ θεῶν χοροποί᾽ ἄναξ, ὅπως μοι Μύσια Κνώσι᾽ ὀρ-
(contd.)   Anacreontic
Glyconic   Glyconic

χήματ᾽ αὐτοδαῆ ξυνὼν ἰάψῃς· νῦν γὰρ ἐμοὶ μέλει χορεῦσαι.
Anacreontic   Anacreontic

If we ask why Sophocles uses this rhythm here, perhaps we shall find the answer in a fragment of Pindar's :

Pind. *fr.* 95

Glyconic   Glyconic

ὦ Πὰν Ἀρκαδίας μεδέων, καὶ σεμνῶν ἀδύτων φύλαξ. . . .

Glyconic   Glyconic

ματρὸς μεγάλας ὀπαδέ, σεμνᾶν Χαρίτων μέλημα τερπνόν.
Anacreontic   Anacreontic

When Sophocles addresses a hymn to Pan, he writes in the rhythm used by Pindar for the same purpose before him. Possibly, the intention of both was to remind their audiences of a traditional song: or did the song take its shape in reminiscence of the poets? For it is in the same rhythm :

Scolium 5, Bergk III p. 644

Glyconic

ὦ Πὰν Ἀρκαδίας μεδέων κλεεννᾶς,
Anacreontic

Glyconic

ὀρχηστά, Βρομίαις ὀπαδὲ Νύμφαις,
Anacreontic

† γελασίαις † ὦ Πὰν ἐπ᾽ ἐμαῖς

Glyconic   Glyconic

εὐφροσύναισι, ταῖσδ᾽ ἀοιδαῖς κεχαρημένος . . .
Anacreontic

Rhythmical effects such as these—and surely they are very beautiful—are not to be found, so far as I know, in the poetry of any other language. No doubt, Greek lends itself more easily than most to intricate rhythmical design, but part of the credit must be given to the Greek poets themselves who excelled all others in the subtlety of their sense of rhythm. For it is possible to produce effects—less precise, but similar —in a language which by comparison is so intractable as English:

O be not fearful; as a friend in flight contending to this rock my airy journey have I wing'd.
Eager for this adventure, my father's word hardly I won.
Hither I ride on the flying breezes.
I heard afar off the reverberating echoes in my hollow cave, and unflushed with the shame of maidens
I sped on my chariot-steed unsandall'd.

I see, Prometheus; and a mist of sorrow falleth on my vision, tears are springing to mine eyes
Thus to behold thy beauty by day and night wasted in these
Adamant shackles of shame and torment.
For new the rulers who are throned above in heaven, and the laws of Zeus are new, framed for a harsh dominion.
The mighty of old he hath brought to nothing.

CHAPTER FIVE

MUSICAL FORM IN GREEK POETRY

THE kindred arts of poetry and music differ in one most important respect. Poetry tells a story; like sculpture, it is a representative art. A poem often takes its shape from the impress of its subject-matter—for every story has a beginning and an end—and thus assumes a natural coherence which diminishes the necessity of an artificial form. Music, on the other hand, tells no story; like architecture, it is a non-representative art. Not being a direct narrative of human experience, it depends for its coherence upon a superimposed, artistic form, which will appeal to the aesthetic instincts of the hearer and convey to him a proper sense of unity and completeness. It is only natural, therefore, that conscious artistic form should have been more highly developed by musicians, for whom it is indispensable, than by poets, for whom it is not. And it reaches its highest development in the hands of those composers whose work is furthest removed from direct representation of human experience—in the fugues of Bach, the quartets of Mozart, the symphonies of Beethoven, which cannot be fully appreciated without previous acquaintance with the formal principles underlying their composition.

TWO-PART FORM   We saw that the simplest kind of musical sentence owes its coherence to a natural response by which the second of its component phrases provides a complement or counterpart to the first. The same principle underlies the simplest kind of musical design, known among musicians as *Two-part* form. If we listen to *God Save the King*, for example, we find that, both rhythmically and melodically, the design falls into two more or less equal portions, the second being a restatement, in similar though not identical terms, of the first. This is

Two-part form: and, for convenience, we may represent it
by the symbol A–B.

Musicians felt the need of a design which would offer them THREE-
greater scope than is afforded by simple Two-part form. Hence PART
the rise of what is called *Three-part* form. Listen to a stanza FORM
of *The Red Flag*, and you will find that the composition falls
not into two but into three parts, the third being a restatement of the first, and the second something in the nature of
a digression or development. Statement—digression—restatement. First subject—second subject—first subject. The design
may be described in various ways, or symbolically A–B–A.
Minuet-and-trio form is based on this principle. The first piece MINUET
of the design, the minuet, begins with a first subject which AND
develops into a second, and it ends by returning to the first. RONDO
The second piece, the Trio, is constructed in the same way,
and the third is a repetition of the first.

A. Minuet: A–B–A.

B. Trio: A–B–A.

A. Minuet: A–B–A.

The Rondo is a further elaboration of the same principle.
In the Simple Rondo the first subject is repeated twice—in
the middle and at the end; but the first and second statements
of it, and the second and third, are separated by two digressions
or episodes, thus: A–B–A–C–A. The Sonata-Rondo is even
more elaborate. There are two subjects and a central episode.
The first subject is followed by the second, then the first
recurs; in the middle comes the episode; then the first subject returns, then the second, and finally the first again:
A–B–A–C–A–B–A.

Sometimes, the completion of the design by the return to THE
the opening subject is followed by an extension or appendage, CODA
added either to soften a too abrupt conclusion or to provide
a sort of epilogue in which the main themes of the composition
are summarised. This is the *coda*.

The superior flexibility of Three-part over Two-part form
may be seen from its use in continuous composition, where
the second subject of one piece of the design is sometimes
taken up as the first subject of the next: A–B–A, B–C–B,
C–D–C, etc. This is Cyclic form, and reminds us of the *terza
rima* of *The Divine Comedy*, in which the first verse of each
terzetta rhymes with the third, and the second with the first
and third of the next *terzetta* :

> La gloria di colui che tutto move
> per l'universo penetra, e risplende
> in una parte più e meno altrove.
> Nel ciel che più della sua luce prende
> fu' io ; e vidi cose che ridire
> nè sa nè può qual di lassù discende.

Of course, it must not be supposed that these formal principles are rules which the composer is bound rigidly to observe:
they are merely the fundamental laws, based on aesthetic
instinct, which form the groundwork of his art. He is free
to vary them as much as he chooses: only, even when he
diverges from them, his work cannot be rightly understood
without reference to these original types.

That the Greek poets were endowed with a finer sense of
form than most poets of modern times, will hardly be denied.
Nor is it difficult to see how they came by this highly developed sense of form: they were also musicians. Mr Sheppard
has shown by a detailed study of the structural form of Greek
poetry, how, in epic, lyric and tragedy alike, they strove to
attain a formal unity by the artistic arrangement of episodes,
images and ideas[1]. The principles of composition which he
discovered by a study of the subject-matter alone are essenti-
ally the same as those which underlie the form of modern
music. We shall have more to say on this important subject
later; for the moment, let us note the parallel, and remember

---

[1] J. T. Sheppard, *Pattern of the Iliad* (1922). See also *Aeschylus and Sophocles*
(1927), *Cambridge Ancient History*, vol. v, chap. v, and his articles in *J.H.S.*
(1922), pp. 220 ff., *C.R.* (1922), pp. 5–11.

that nothing is more natural than that poets who were also musicians should have revealed in their poetry a musical technique.

One link is still wanting to make our argument complete. Musical composition is based on certain fundamental principles of artistic form; and we have evidence that these principles underlie the formal technique evolved by the Greek poets. Can they be traced in their rhythms? To answer this question we must examine a unit in the rhythmical design larger than any we have noticed so far—the strophe.

In some songs written in Three-part form—in *The Red Flag* for example—the rhythm of the words is the same throughout: the musical form depends on variations in the melody alone. In others, however, the form is reflected in rhythm and melody alike. In Schumann's *Freisinn*, for instance, the second subject begins with a change of rhythm— a change which is reflected in the words themselves.

A. Lasst mich nur auf meinem Sattel gelten,
    Bleibt in euren Hütten, euren Zelten,
    Und ich reite froh in alle Ferne,
    Ueber meine Mütze nur die Sterne.

B. Er hat euch die Gestirne gesetzt
    Als Leiter zu Land und See,
    Damit er euch daran ergötzt,
    Stets blickend in die Höh'.

A. Lasst mich nur, etc.

Now the melody of Greek music has perished, but the rhythm has survived. In many pieces, the rhythm is the same from beginning to end, and their musical form, if they had a musical form, has perished along with the melodies which accompanied them. In others the rhythm varies. Let us examine these with a view to discovering on what principle the rhythms are built up.

Starting from the isolated foot, we advanced, through the figure and phrase, to the sentence. We now come to the strophe—the recurrent group of sentences which constitutes

THE
GREEK
STROPHE

the framework of the poem as a whole. Strophic lyric is of three kinds—monostrophic, antistrophic and triadic. The monostrophic poem falls into a number of single strophes, each identical in rhythmical form. The antistrophic poem falls into pairs of strophes: no two pairs are alike, while the strophe and antistrophe of which each pair is composed are identical. In the triadic poem, strophe and antistrophe are followed by an epode, which differs from them in form, though similar in its general character: and this tripartite design is repeated without variation in detail or in the order of its parts. Thus, in the first two kinds it is the strophe, in the third the triad, which is the organic unit—the largest the poem contains. Here, if anywhere, we shall expect to find traces of formal design. And since, for the reason explained above, these traces are less likely to appear in homogeneous rhythm than in heterogeneous, let us begin with some simple examples of Two-part form in homogeneous Dorian.

STROPHES
IN TWO-
PART
FORM

Aesch. *Pers.* 854–99[1].

Str. 1

A ὦ πόποι, ἦ μεγάλας ἀγαθᾶς τε πολισσονόμου βιοτᾶς ἐπε-
κύρσαμεν, εὖθ' ὁ γηραιὸς

B πανταρκής, ἀκάκης, ἄμαχος βασιλεύς, ἰσόθεος Δαρεῖος ἆρχε
χώρας.

Str. 2

A ὅσσας δ' εἷλε πόλεις πόρον οὐ διαβὰς "Αλυος ποταμοῖο, οὐδ'
ἀφ' ἑστίας συθείς,

B οἶαι Στρυμονίου πελάγους 'Αχελωΐδες εἰσὶ πάροικοι Θρη-
κίων ἐπαύλων.

Str. 3

A νᾶσοί θ' αἳ κατὰ πρῶν' ἅλιον περίκλυστοι τᾷδε γᾷ προσή-
μεναι,

---

[1] This free form of Dorian is Stesichorean: see W. Headlam, *J.H.S.* vol. xxii, p. 215; and cf. below, pp. 103–4. Its peculiar characteristic—the long dactylic phrase—is obtained by resolution of the final spondee of the prosodiac.

B οἷα Λέσβος, ἐλαιόφυτός τε Σάμος, Χίος ἠδὲ Πάρος, Νάξος,

Μύκονος, Τήνῳ τε συνάπτουσ᾽ Ἄνδρος ἀγχιγείτων.

All these sentences are of the same type—a long dactylic announcement, followed by an epitritic or trochaic responsion. And each strophe consists of two such sentences.

Eur. *Andr.* 766–76

A ἢ μὴ γενοίμαν ἢ πατέρων ἀγαθῶν
εἴην πολυκτήτων τε δόμων μέτοχος.
εἴ τι γὰρ πάσχοι τις ἀμήχανον, ἀλκᾶς
οὐ σπάνις εὐγενέταις,

B κηρυσσομένοισι δ᾽ ἀπ᾽ ἐσθλῶν δωμάτων
τιμὰ καὶ κλέος· οὗτοι λείψανα τῶν ἀγαθῶν
ἀνδρῶν ἀφαιρεῖται χρόνος· ἁ δ᾽ ἀρετὰ
καὶ θανοῦσι λάμπει.

Both sentences are quadruple; but in this case the responsions are different. The Two-part character of the whole, however, is perfectly clear.

Pindar elaborates this simple form by the addition of a *coda*: THE
Pind. *N.* ix 1–5   CODA

A Κωμάσομεν παρ᾽ Ἀπόλλωνος Σεκυωνόθε, Μοῖσαι,
τὰν νεοκτίσταν ἐς Αἴτναν, ἔνθ᾽ ἀναπεπταμέναι ξείνων νενίκ-
ανται θύραι,

B ὄλβιον ἐς Χρομίου δῶμ᾽. ἀλλ᾽ ἐπέων γλυκὺν ὕμνον πράσσετε.
τὸ κρατήσιππον γὰρ ἐς ἅρμ᾽ ἀναβαίνων ματέρι καὶ διδύμοις
παίδεσσιν αὐδὰν μανύει

C Πυθῶνος αἰπεινᾶς ὁμοκλάροις ἐπόπταις.

The first two sentences both end with a double epitrite
($\underline{}\cup\underline{}\underline{}\cup\underline{}$); the third, the *coda*, is composed of three epitrites —a common conclusion to Dorian periods known as the Στησι- χορεῖον[1].

A clear example of Two-part form in Ionian rhythm will be found in a strophe already quoted from *The Suppliants* of

---

[1] Another example of two-part form with coda will be found in the twelfth Pythian.

40   GREEK LYRIC METRE

Aeschylus (1029–36)¹. The first sentence concludes with a
ditrochee, the second with an Anacreontic; and in both the
length of the announcing phrase is the same. Another, in
heterogeneous rhythm, will be found in the strophe from the
Prometheus analysed at the end of the last chapter (*P.V.*
130–40)². Here, the announcement is Anacreontic and iambo-
choriambic, the responsion an Aeolian decasyllable; and both
sentences are similar, except that the second is more condensed.
We shall come across many more strophes of this type when
we examine the plays of Aeschylus in detail.

STROPHES   Three-part form may be seen at its simplest in a strophe
IN THREE- like the following, where the first phrase is repeated after a
PART   short digression:
FORM

Aesch. *Agam.* 1135–41 (Dochmiac)

A φρενομανής τις εἶ θεοφόρητος, ἀμφὶ δ' αὐτᾶς θροεῖς
B νόμον ἄνομον. οἷά τις ξουθὰ
   ἀκόρετος βοᾶς, φεῦ, ταλαίναις φρεσὶν
A Ἴτυν Ἴτυν στένουσ' ἀμφιθαλῆ κακοῖς ἀηδὼν βίον.

More commonly, however, the restatement of the opening
subject is shorter than its first occurrence:

Aesch. *Agam.* 170–7. A Trochaic: B Dactylic

A Ζεὺς ὅστις ποτ' ἐστίν, εἰ τόδ' αὐτῷ φίλον κεκλημένῳ, τοῦτό
   νιν προσεννέπω. οὐδ' ἔχω προσεικάσαι πάντ' ἐπισταθμώμενος
B πλὴν Διός, εἰ τὸ μάταν ἀπὸ φροντίδος ἄχθος
A χρὴ βαλεῖν ἐτητύμως.

Nor need the formal divisions be coterminous with the sentences. In the passage which follows they are independent:

Aesch. *Supp.* 638–46. A Aeolian: B Paeonic.

νῦν ὅτε καὶ θεοὶ Διογενεῖς κλύοιτ' εὐκταῖα γένει χεούσας·
(A) Tripody   Pherecratic   Pherecratic

¹ See above, p. 14.   ² See above, p. 30.

μήποτε πυρίφατον τάνδε Πελασγίαν τὸν ἄχορον βοᾶν
——————————— ——————————— ————————
Tripody   Tripody   (B) Dochmiac

κτίσαι μάχλον Ἄρη
————————
Dochmiac

τὸν ἀρότοις θερίζοντα βροτοὺς ἐν ἄλλοις.
———————— ————————————
Dochmiac   (A) Pherecratic

In a few cases, we find that the Greek poets developed Three-part form somewhat on the lines of the modern Rondo. In the strophe which follows, the three main subjects are trochaic, dactylic and dochmiac, with cretic as a link between the first and third:

Aesch. *Agam.* 966–77[1]. A Trochaic: B Dactylic: C Dochmiac. **DEVELOP-**
Form: A–B–A–C–A.   **MENT OF**
                                                              THREE-
τίπτε μοι τόδ' ἐμπέδως δεῖμα προστατήριον   **PART**
————————————————————————————   **FORM**
A

καρδίας τερασκόπου ποτᾶται,
——————————————————
A

μαντιπολεῖ δ' ἀκέλευστος ἄμισθος ἀοιδά,
—————————————————————————
B

οὐδ' ἀποπτύσας δίκαν δυσκρίτων ὀνειράτων
—————————————————————————
A

θάρσος εὐπειθὲς ἵζει φρενὸς φίλον θρόνον;
————————   ——————————————
(cretics)   A

χρόνος δ' ἐπεὶ πρυμνησίων ξυνεμβολὰς ψαμμὰς ἀκτὰ παρή-
—————— ——————————————— ————————
C   A   (cretics)

φησεν, εὖθ' ὑπ' Ἴλιον ὦρτο ναυβάτας στρατός.
——————————————————————————
A

No poet was more skilful in his development of Three-part form than Pindar. So let us conclude this account of strophic composition with an analysis of three of his odes, which will illustrate almost all the metrical principles I have hitherto enunciated.

————————————
[1] 974–5 ξυνεμβολὰς ψαμμὰς ἀκτὰ παρήφησεν Headlam: ξυνεμβόλοις' ψαμμὰς ἀκάτα παρήβησεν.

Pind. *P*. vi. Monostrophic. A Paeonic : B Aeolian.

Form : A–B–A–B–A–B–A.

(A) Dochmiac

Ἀκούσατ'· ἢ γὰρ ἑλικώπιδος Ἀφροδίτας ἄρουραν ἢ Χαρίτων

_____(B) Pherecratic_____Tripody with anacrusis

(paeon)   (A) Dochmiac   Link

ἀναπολίζομεν,ὄμφαλον ἐρίβρόμου χθονὸς ἐς νάϊον προσοιχόμενοι·

Tripody   (B) Glyconic

Πυθιόνικος ἔνθ' ὀλβίοισιν Ἐμμενίδαις

Tripody   Glyconic

(paeon)   (A) Dochmiac

ποταμίᾳ τ' Ἀκράγαντι καὶ μὰν Ξενοκράτει

Tripody

Dochmiac

ἑτοῖμος ὕμνων θησαυρὸς ἐν πολυχρύσῳ

_____(B) Pherecratic

(A) Dochmiac

Ἀπολλωνίᾳ τετείχισται νάπᾳ.

Pind. *P*. v. Triadic. A Paeonic : B Aeolian. There is also
a recurrent figure ⏑⏑⏑⏑ or ⏑⏑. Form of strophe : A–B–A–
B–A–B–A–B–A. Form of epode : A–B–A–B–A–B–A–B–A–
B–A.

Str.

(A) Dochmiac   Dochmiac

Ὁ πλοῦτος εὐρυσθενής, ὅταν τις ἀρετᾷ κεκραμένον καθαρᾷ

_____(B) Glyconic

(A) Dochmiac   (A) Paeon

βροτήσιος ἀνὴρ πότμου παραδόντος αὐτὸν ἀνάγῃ

_____(B) Glyconic

Dochmiac

πολύφιλον ἐπέταν.

Paeon   (⏑⏑⏑)   Dochmiac   (⏑⏑)

ὦ θεόμορ' Ἀρκεσίλα, σύ τοί νιν κλυτᾶς αἰῶνος

ἀκρᾶν βαθμίδων ἄπο

(B) Tripody with anacrusis

(A) Dochmiac
σὺν εὐδοξίᾳ μετανίσεαι
(B) Tripody

(A) Dochmiac
ἔκατι χρυσαρμάτου Κάστορος·

Cretic (‒◡◡‒)　　Paeon & Cretic
εὐδίαν ὃς μετὰ χειμέριον ὄμβρον τεὰν

Dochmiac
καταιθύσσει μάκαιραν ἑστίαν.

Ep.

(A) Bacchius & Paeon
Ἀπολλώνιον ἄθυρμα. τῷ σε μὴ λαθέτω
(B) Glyconic

(A) Dochmiac
Κυράνας γλυκὺν ἀμφὶ κᾶπον Ἀφροδίτας ἀειδόμενον,
Anaclastic Glyconic　　　　　　(B) Tripody

παντὶ μὲν θεὸν αἴτιον ὑπερτιθέμεν,
Tripody　　　　Tripody

(A) Dochmiac
φιλεῖν δὲ Κάρρωτον ἔξοχ' ἑταίρων·
(B) Pherecratic

(A) Paeon (‒◡◡‒)　　　　　　　　　(A) Cretic
ὃς οὐ τὰν Ἐπιμαθέος ἄγων ὀψινόου θυγατέρᾱ πρόφασιν Βαττιδᾶν
Anaclastic Tripody　　　　　　(B) Tripody

Dochmiac　　Dochmiac　　Cretics
ἀφίκετο δόμους θεμισκρεόντων· ἀλλ' ἀρισθάρματον

(A) Dochmiac
ὕδατι Κασταλίας ξενωθεὶς γέρας ἀμφέβαλε τεαῖσιν κόμαις.
(B) Glyconic　　　　Glyconic[1]

Pind. N. vii. Triadic. A Aeolian: B Aeolian and Paeonic
combined. There are also some dochmiac and iambic figures.
Form of strophe: A–B–A. Form of epode: the same.

[1] ‒◡◡‒◡‒◡‒‒ for ‒◡◡‒◡‒◡‒‒.

The principal phrases are as follows:

A (1) ⌣⏒ ⏒⌣⌣ ⏒⌣ ⏒⏑
    ⏒⌣ ⏒⌣⌣ ⏒⌣ ⏒⏑ } Enneasyllables
    ⏒⌣⌣ ⏒⌣ ⏒⌣ ⏒⏑ }

(2) ⌣ ⌣⌣⌣ ⏒⌣⌣ ⏒⌣ ⏒⏑ Decasyllable with anacrusis[1]

(3) ⌣⌣⌣ ⏒⌣⌣ ⏒⌣ ⏒ Glyconic

(4) ⏒⌣⌣ ⏒⌣ ⊚⏑ }
    ⌣⌣⌣ ⏒⌣⌣ ⏑⏑ } Pherecratics

(5) ⏑ ⏒⌣⌣ ⏒⌣ ⏒ Tripody with anacrusis

(6) ⏒⌣⌣ ⏒⌣ ⌣⌣⌣ ⏒⌣ ⏒⏑ Hendecasyllable

B (7) ⏑ ⏒⌣⌣ ⏒⌣ ⏒ / ⌣⌣⌣ ⌣⌣⌣ ⏒⌣ ⏒

(8) ⏑⏒⌣⌣ ⏒⌣ ⏒ / ⌣⌣⌣⏒ ⌣⏒

(9) ⊚⌣ ⏒⌣⌣ ⏒ / ⌣⌣⌣⏒ ⌣⏒

Str.

(A) 1   Iambic
Ἐλείθυια, πάρεδρε Μοιρᾶν βαθυφρόνων,

6
παῖ μεγαλοσθενέος, ἄκουσον, Ἥρας, γενέτειρα τέκνων·
              4
Iambic
ἄνευ σέθεν

4   Iambic   Dochmiac
οὐ φάος, οὐ μέλαιναν δρακέντες εὐφρόναν τεὰν ἀδελφεὰν

2   Link   Iambic
ἐλάχομεν ἀγλαόγυιον Ἥβαν. ἀναπνέομεν δ' οὐχ ἅπαντες ἐπὶ ϝίσα.
                    a

(B) 7
εἴργει δὲ πότμῳ ζυγένθ' ἕτερον ἕτερα. σὺν δὲ τὶν
          a echoed

8
καὶ παῖς ὁ Θεαρίωνος ἀρετᾷ κριθεὶς

(A) 5   1
εὔδοξος ἀείδεται Σωγένης μετὰ πενταέθλοις.

[1] Cf. Pind. O. xiv, 1, Καφισίων ὑδάτων λαχοῖσαι. But the analysis of ἐλάχομεν is doubtful. It may stand for a dactyl.

Ep.

(A) 4
σοφοὶ δὲ μέλλοντα τριταῖον ἄνεμον
Dochmiac   b

4   Iambus
ἔμαθον, οὐδ' ὑπὸ κέρδει βλάβεν·
   b echoed

(B) 9
ἀφνεὸς πενιχρός τε θανάτου πέρας

9
ἅμα νέονται· ἐγὼ δὲ πλέον' ἔλπομαι

(A) 3   I
λόγον Ὀδυσσέος ἢ πάθαν διὰ τὸν ἀδυεπῆ γενέσθ' Ὅμηρον.
c   c echoed

To reduce these beautiful and intricate rhythmical designs
to a paper analysis is a difficult and not altogether satisfactory
task. Rhythmical composition is a flexible, delicate art, and
cannot be adequately presented except through its proper
medium—oral recitation. The arbiter must always be the ear,
not the eye; and it is not easy to appeal to the ear through
the eye. Therefore, I ask the reader, after studying the analyses
given above, to recite the words of the poet aloud for himself,
and to consider whether, guided by the principles of phrasing
and of composition which have been laid down, he does not
find in them a natural, organic unity appealing directly to his
ear and to his sense of form.

CHAPTER SIX

SIGNIFICANT RHYTHM

I SUGGESTED at the beginning of the last chapter that, by comparison with poetry, music was a non-representative art—an abstraction or sublimation rather than a direct description of human experience. But this is not equally true of all music. Even in modern Europe, where the art has attained its highest development, we have, along with the fugues of Bach and the symphonies of Beethoven, the music-dramas of Wagner. Operatic music is not complete in itself: though still mistress over poetry, it is the servant of the drama, and in virtue of that relationship it assumes certain features which distinguish it from music of the purer and more abstract kind. Different combinations of melody and rhythm produce different emotional associations; and out of this property of music Wagner contrives to create many of his most striking dramatic effects. Wotan, Brünnhilde, Siegfried—not only do we see these figures on the stage, we hear them in the music, and so can be reminded of them through our ears when they are no longer visible to our eyes. Fate, Love, and Death—the Ring, the Sword, the Curse—all these themes have their appropriate musical *Leit-motives*, which are so skilfully woven into the dramatic texture as to provide, as it were, a running musical commentary on the varying fortunes of gods and heroes displayed to us on the stage.

THE *LEIT-MOTIV*

Greek music, in general, did not exist for its own sake, and perhaps its most important function was to provide an appropriate accompaniment to drama and the dance. In this respect, it was more closely related to the operatic music of Wagner than to the abstract music of Bach and Beethoven. Hence we are not surprised to find that the Greeks attached the greatest importance to the emotional associations—the ἦθος—of the different modes. The Dorian mode was solemn, manly, characteristically Greek. The Ionian was relaxed, effeminate—there was something un-Greek about it. The Lydian was voluptuous, the Phrygian exciting and passionate[1]. All this is a matter of common knowledge: but what we have now to consider is whether similar ethical significances were attached to the different classes of rhythm—that is to say, whether the ethical quality of a piece of Greek music depended on the kind of rhythm, as well as upon the kind of melody, in which it was composed. For an answer to this question we must turn to the poets themselves, and in particular to the dramatists, who change their rhythms incessantly, and may be expected to have some reason for doing so.

The characteristic Dorian virtues, associated in the minds of the Greeks with the Dorian mode, were ἀρετά, εὐσέβεια, σωφροσύνα. For this reason, Aristotle held that the Dorian mode was the most suitable for purposes of education[2]. He also wrote a hymn to 'Αρετά. We may presume that he wrote it in the Dorian mode: we know that he wrote it in the Dorian rhythm:

Arist. (Bergk II pp. 360-2)

Prosodiac

'Αρετά, πολύμοχθε γένει βροτείῳ, θήραμα κάλλιστον βίῳ,

σᾶς πέρι, παρθένε, μορφᾶς

καὶ θανεῖν ζαλωτὸς ἐν 'Ελλάδι πότμος

καὶ πόνους τλῆναι μαλερούς ἀκάμαντας.

Hesiod had said that 'Αρετά dwelt upon a rocky height[3]. Simonides recalled the theme of the epic poet in a lyrical setting; and he used the Dorian rhythm:

Simon. 58

ἔστι τις λόγος ποτὲ τὰν 'Αρετὰν

ναίειν δυσαμβάτοις ἐπὶ πέτραις,

---

[1] For references see below, p. 67 n.
[2] Arist. Pol. 1342 A.   [3] Hes. Op. 284-90.

νῦν δέ μιν θεῶν χῶρον ἁγνὸν ἀμφέπειν
οὐδ᾽ ἀπαντᾶν βλεφάροις θνατῶν ἔσοπτον,
ᾧ μὴ δακέθυμος ἱδρὼς ἔνδοθεν μόλῃ θ᾽, ἵκηταί τ᾽ ἐς ἄκρον
ἀνδρείας . . .

The Chorus of the *Andromache* extol the virtue that comes of noble birth in a strophe which has already been quoted as an example of Dorian rhythm[1], and ends:

οὗτοι λείψανα τῶν ἀγαθῶν
ἀνδρῶν ἀφαιρεῖται χρόνος· ἁ δ᾽ ἀρετὰ
καὶ θανοῦσι λάμπει.

The Chorus of the *Medea* declare that the course of over-passionate love runs counter to virtue and good fame:

Eur. *Med.* 627–41 (Dorian)

ἔρωτες ὑπὲρ μὲν ἄγαν ἐλθόντες οὐκ εὐδοξίαν
οἰδ᾽ ἀρετὰν παρέδωκαν ἄνδρασιν . . .
στέργοι δέ με σωφροσύνα, δώρημα κάλλιστον θεῶν[2].

In the *Oedipus Tyrannus* the Theban elders pray, in Dorian rhythm, for purity of word and action—for εὐσέβεια:

Soph. *O. T.* 863–5

εἴ μοι ξυνείη φέροντι μοῖρα τὰν εὔσεπτον ἁγνείαν λόγων
ἔργων τε πάντων ὧν νόμοι πρόκεινται. . .

DORIAN FOR THE GREEKS

We observed that the Dorian was felt to be the most Greek of the modes. In the same way, the Dorian rhythm seems to have been used in preference to others by the poets for narrating the exploits of the Greek race, or for the contrast of Greek with Asiatic. Stesichorus used it for his poem on the sack of Troy:

Stesich. 18

ᾤκτειρε γὰρ αὐτὸν ὕδωρ αἰεὶ φορέοντα Διὸς κούρα βασιλεῦσιν.

---

[1] Eur. *Andr.* 766–801: see above, p. 39.

[2] For other examples of Dorian for Ἀρετά, see Eur. *I. A.* 562–3, *Hel.* 1151–4, fr. 11 Nauck; Mel. fr. adesp. 104 B οὐ μήποτε τὰν ἀρετὰν ἀλλάξομαι ἀντ᾽ ἀδίκου κέρδεος.

Aeschylus treated the same subject in the same rhythm:

Aesch. *Agam.* 104–5¹

κύριός εἰμι θροεῖν ὅδιον κράτος αἴσιον ἀνδρῶν

ἐκτελέων . . .

The same theme was a favourite with Euripides, and the rhythm is usually Dorian:

Eur. *Hec.* 928–32

κέλευσμα δ᾽ ἦν κατ᾽ ἄστυ Τροίας τόδ᾽ · ˜Ω παῖδες Ἑλλά-
_____
Iambic   Dorian . . .

νων, πότε δὴ πότε τὰν Ἰλιάδα σκοπιὰν

πέρσαντες ἥξετ᾽ οἴκους;

Ibid. 905–9

σὺ μέν, ὦ πατρὶς Ἰλιάς, τῶν ἀπορθήτων πόλις οὐκέτι λέξῃ·
_____
Ionian   Dorian . . .

τοῖον Ἑλλάνων νέφος ἀμφί σε κρύπτει δορὶ δὴ δορὶ πέρσαν.

In the next passage the effect of the Dorian is enforced by a happy contrast with Aeolian:

Eur. *I. A.* 751–5

ἥξει δὴ Σιμόεντα καὶ δίνας ἀργυροειδεῖς
_____
Aeolian couplet²

ἄγυρις Ἑλλάνων στρατιᾶς ἀνά τε ναυσὶν καὶ σὺν ὅπλοις
_____
Dorian . . .

Ἴλιον ἐς τὸ Τροίας.
_____
Aeolian

The Chorus of the *Andromache* are Greeks, Andromache herself is a Trojan. When the Chorus come to comfort her, they sing in the rhythm which befits their nationality:

Eur. *Andr.* 117–34³

ὦ γύναι, ἃ Θέτιδος δάπεδον καὶ ἀνάκτορα θάσσεις
_____

δαρὸν οὐδὲ λείπεις,
_____

¹ See below, p. 104.
² Cf. Aesch. *Agam.* 699–700 κελσάντων Σιμόεντος ἀκτὰς ἐπ᾽ ἀεξιφύλλους.
³ Here we have two examples of the prosodiac with final dactyl: ⏑⏑ ⏑⏑ ⏑⏑
for ⏑⏑ ⏑⏑ ⏑⏑. See Appendix for other examples.

Φθιὰς ὅμως ἔμολον ποτὶ σὰν Ἀσιήτιδα γένναν,
εἴ τί σοι δυναίμαν . . .

—FOR ZEUS

Lastly, no doubt because of its connotation of σεμνότης and of its peculiarly Greek character, the Dorian rhythm seems to have been consecrated to the name of Zeus:

Aesch. *P. V.* 542–60

μηδάμ' ὁ πάντα νέμων θεῖτ' ἐμᾷ γνώμᾳ κράτος ἀντίπαλον Ζεύς.

The Ocean nymphs have already expressed, in mournful measures, their compassion for the suffering Titan. They now turn to address to Zeus a solemn hymn in which they preach the necessity of submission to his will. The change of subject, impressive enough in itself, is made doubly so by the change of rhythm. So, in *The Suppliants*, the daughters of Danaus, after lamenting their plight in Ionian strains, remind themselves that the ways of Zeus are dark and past searching out:

Aesch. *Supp.* 88–90[1]

εἴθ' εἴη Διὸς εὖ παναλήθως—Διὸς ἵμερος οὐκ
εὐθήρατος ἐτύχθη.

In the *Choephoroe* Orestes and Electra begin their invocation over their father's tomb with a lament, and the metre is Aeolian; but they go on to pray for vengeance, and their voices become more passionate. The brother cries:

Aesch. *Cho.* 379–81[2]

τοῦτο διαμπερέως ἵκεθ' ἅπερ τι βέλος· Ζεῦ,Ζεῦ κάτωθεν ἰάλλων.
Prosodiacs ‖ Pherecratic

The sister echoes his cry:

Ibid. 393–4

καί ποτ' ἂν ἀμφιθαλὴς Ζεὺς ἐπὶ χεῖρα βάλοι.

By a natural extension of idea, Dorian rhythm came to be associated not only with Zeus, but with the offspring of Zeus,

---

[1] 88 εἴθ' εἴη Headlam: εἰθείη.
[2] 379 διαμπερέως Headlam: διαμπερὲς οὖς.

divine and mortal, when the poet had their lofty origin in mind. The Theban elders address the Voice of Zeus made manifest at Delphi:

Soph. *O. T.* 151–67

ὦ Διὸς ἀδυεπὲς Φάτι, τίς ποτε τᾶς πολυχρύσου
  Πυθῶνος ἀγλαὰς ἔβας
Θήβας; ἐκτέταμαι φοβερὰν φρένα δείματι πάλλων.

They go on to invoke the daughter of Zeus, Athena: —FOR ATHENA

πρῶτά σε κεκλόμενος, θύγατερ Διός, ἄμβροτ' 'Αθάνα . . .

The sailors of Salamis ascribe their leader's reported madness —FOR ARTEMIS
to the intervention of Artemis, daughter of Zeus:

Soph. *Aj.* 172–91

ἦ ῥά σε Ταυροπόλα Διὸς "Αρτεμις, ὦ μεγάλα φάτις, ὦ μᾶτερ
  αἰσχύνας ἐμᾶς,
ὥρμασε πανδάμους ἐπὶ βοῦς ἀγελαίας . . .

And they pray to Zeus and Apollo to prove the report untrue: —FOR APOLLO

καὶ γὰρ ἂν θεία νόσος· ἀλλ' ἀπερύκοι
καὶ Ζεὺς κακὰν καὶ Φοῖβος 'Αργείων φάτιν.

The old men of Colonus entreat Zeus and his holy child Athena to grant the Athenians victory in battle:

Soph. *O. C.* 1085–95[1]

ἰὼ θεῶν πάνταρχε, παντόπτα Ζεῦ, πόροις γᾶς τᾶσδε δαμού-
χοις σθένει 'πινικείῳ τὸν εὔαγρον τελειῶσαι λόχον,
σεμνά τε παῖς Παλλὰς 'Αθάνα.

The Trojans pray for victory to Apollo as son of Zeus, in the same rhythm:

---

[1] For Dorian for Zeus and Athena, cf. also Mel. fr. adesp. 82 A–B Bergk (III p. 710) κλῦθί μοι Ζανός τε κούρη Ζανί τ' ἐλευθερίῳ: Lamprocles 1 Bergk (III pp. 554–5).

Eur. *Rh.* 224-41

Θυμβραῖε καὶ Δάλιε καὶ Λυκίας ναὸν ἐμβατεύων

Ἄπολλον, ὦ Δία κεφαλά, μόλε τοξήρης, ἱκοῦ ἐννύχιος

καὶ γενοῦ σωτήριος ἀνέρι πομπᾶς

ἀγεμὼν καὶ ξύλλαβε Δαρδανίδαις,

ὦ παγκρατές, ὦ Τροίας τείχη παλαιὰ δείμας.

The votaries of Tauric Artemis praise Apollo, son of Zeus by Leto, in the same measure:

Eur. *I. T.* 1234-5[1]

εὖπαις ὁ Λατοῦς γόνος, τόν ποτε Δηλιὰς ἐν

καρποφόροις γυάλοις ἔτικτε . . .

—FOR EPAPHUS   Epaphus, the offspring of Io, was begotten by Zeus. So the Danaids invoke the aid of their divine ancestor in Dorian:

Aesch. *Supp.* 40-57

νῦν δ' ἐπικεκλομένα Δῖον πόρτιν ὑπερπόντιον τιμάορ' ἶνιν . . .

Zeus begot Perseus of Danae, visiting her in a shower of gold:

Soph. *Ant.* 944-50

ἔτλα καὶ Δανάας οὐράνιον φῶς

ἀλλάξαι δέμας ἐν χαλκοδέτοις αὐλαῖς·

κρυπτομένα δ' ἐν τυμβήρει θαλάμῳ κατεζεύχθη.

                                  Pherecratic protracted[2]

καίτοι καὶ γενεᾷ τίμιος, ὦ παῖ παῖ,

καὶ Ζηνὸς ταμιεύεσκε γόνους χρυσορύτους.

—FOR HERACLES   Heracles, the greatest of Dorian heroes, was the son of Zeus by Alcmena: and Dorian is used for Heracles both by Sophocles—

---

[1] Cf. Pind. *fr.* 87-88 Χαῖρ' ὦ θεοδμάτα λιπαροπλοκάμου παίδεσσι Λατοῦς ἱμεροέστατον ἔρνος.

[2] Cf. in the same play 816 ἀλλ' Ἀχέροντι νυμφεύσω, 846 ξυμμάρτυρας ὄμμ' ἐπικτῶμαι.

Soph. *Trach.* 94–111

Iambo-choriambic[1]

ὃν αἰόλα Νὺξ ἐναριζομένα τίκτει κατευνάζει τε φλογιζόμενον
Ἄλιον, Ἄλιον αἰτῶ
τοῦτο καρῦξαι τὸν Ἀλκμήνας, πόθι μοι πόθι μοι παῖς
ναίει ποτ', ὦ λαμπρᾷ στεροπᾷ φλεγέθων,
ἢ ποντίας αὐλῶνας ἢ δισσαῖσιν ἀπείροις κλιθείς,
εἴπ' ὦ κρατιστεύων κατ' ὄμμα.

and by Euripides:

Eur. *H. F.* 798–806

ὦ λέκτρων δύο συγγενεῖς εὐναί, θνατογενοῦς τε καὶ
Aeolian
Διός, ὃς ἦλθεν ἐς εὐνὰν Νύμφας τᾶς Περσηΐδος· ὡς
πιστόν μοι τὸ παλαιὸν ἤδη λέχος, ὦ Ζεῦ, σὸν ἐπ' οὐκ
                    Dorian . . .
ἐλπίδι φάνθη, λαμπρὰν δ' ἔδειξ' ὁ χρόνος τὰν Ἡρακλέος ἀλκάν.

Helen was the daughter of Zeus by Leto. Stesichorus —FOR
sought to appease her in Dorian rhythm: HELEN

Stesich. 32

οὐκ ἔστ' ἔτυμος λόγος οὗτος·
οὐδ' ἔβας ἐν ναυσὶν εὐσέλμοις, οὐδ' ἵκεο πέργαμα Τροίας.

When her companions in Egypt assert her divine origin,
they use the same rhythm:

Eur. *Hel.* 1144–6[2]

σὺ Διὸς ἔφυς, ὦ Ἑλένα, θυγάτηρ·
πτανὸς γὰρ ἐν κόλποις σε Λήδας ἐτέκνωσε πατήρ.

The Dioscuri were her brothers. Pindar's hymn to the Twins —FOR
is in Dorian: THE
                                                             DIOSCURI

[1] For this introduction to Dorian cf. below, p. 92.
[2] The analysis of σὺ Διὸς ἔφυς is doubtful: the antistrophe (1158 ᾇ Πριαμίδος) does
not correspond.

Pind. *O.* iii

Τυνδαρίδαις τε φιλοξείνοις ἀδεῖν καλλιπλοκάμῳ θ᾽ Ἑλένᾳ . . .

So was Alcman's:

Alcm. 9

Κάστωρ τε πώλων ὠκέων δματῆρες, ἱππόται σοφοί,
καὶ Πωλυδεύκης κυδρός.

Euripides introduces a touch of Dorian rhythm for the sake of a passing mention of all three together:

Eur. *I. A.* 766–72

εἰρεσίᾳ πελάζῃ Σιμουντίοις ὀχετοῖς
_____
Aeolian

τὰν τῶν ἐν αἰθέρι δισσῶν Διοσκούρων Ἑλέναν
                         _____
                         Epitrite + prosodiac

ἐκ Πριάμου κομίσαι θέλων ἐς γᾶν Ἑλλάδα δοριπόνοις
_____
Aeolian

ἀσπίσι καὶ λόγχαις Ἀχαιῶν.
_____
Prosodiac + epitrite

IONIAN— A CONTRAST TO DORIAN   Dorian, then, stands for the Dorian way of life, for Greece as opposed to Asia, and for the head of the Greek Olympus. All this implies a contrast. We look for other rhythms to represent the Ionian way of life, Asia as opposed to Greece, and other gods less characteristically Greek than Zeus.

IONIC A MINORE FOR LAMENTATION   Let us turn, first of all, to Ionic a minore. Unlike the manly Dorian, it is relaxed and luxuriant in effect—the measure of passionate lamentation, of tearful sighs and groans.

Aesch. *P. V.* 415–16

δακρυσίστακτα δ᾽ ἀπ᾽ ὄσσων ῥαδινῶν λειβομένα ῥέος παρειάν.
_____   _____
Ionic a minore   Anacreontic

Soph. *El.* 826–31[1]

Ἠλ. ἒ ἔ, αἰαῖ. Χο. ὦ παῖ, τί δακρύεις;

Ἠλ. φεῦ. Χο. μηδὲν μέγ᾽ αὔσῃς. Ἠλ. ἀπολεῖς. Χο. πῶς;

_____

[1] It will be noticed in this and the following passages that continuous Ionic a minore is varied by occasional spondees, bacchii and anapaests.

Eur. *Supp.* 42–53

ἐσιδοῦσ' οἰκτρὰ μὲν ὄσσων δάκρυ' ἀμφὶ βλεφάροις, ῥυσὰ δὲ σαρκῶν

πολιᾶν καταδρύμματα χειρῶν· τί γάρ; ἃ φθιμένους παῖδας ἐμοὺς οὔτε δόμους προθέμαν οὔτε τάφων χώματα γαίας ἐσορῶ.

Eur. *Phoen.* 1539–42

τί μ', ὦ παρθένε, βακτρεύμασι τυφλοῦ ποδὸς ἐξάγαγες ἐς φῶς λεχήρη σκοτίων ἐκ θαλάμων οἰκτροτάτοισιν δακρύοισιν . . .

Sappho 62

κατθνάσκει, Κυθέρη', ἄβρος Ἄδωνις, τί κε θεῖμεν; καττύπτεσθε, κόραι, καὶ κατερείκεσθε χίτωνας.

Aeschylus uses Ionic a minore for the lament of the nightingale:

Aesch. *Supp.* 61–3

ὄπα τᾶς Τηρείας μήτιδος οἰκτρᾶς ἀλόχου κιρκηλάτου δ' ἀηδόνος.

Sophocles does the same:

Soph. *Aj.* 627–9

αἴλινον αἴλινον, οὐδ' οἰκτρᾶς γόον ὄρνιθος ἀηδοῦς . . .

The distinctive character of the Ionian way of life is summed up in the word ἁβρότης; and we find that Ionic a minore is the rhythm appropriate to this idea and to the peoples among whom this way of life prevailed. Thus, when Aeschylus wishes to describe Helen, not as the daughter of Zeus, but as she really was—a woman, delicately-veiled, who fired the hearts of men with love, he gives us a touch of Ionic a minore in the musical accompaniment: —FOR ASIATIC LUXURY

Aesch. *Agam.* 692–6

Ἐλέναν; ἐπεὶ πρεπόντως ἐλέναυς ἔλανδρος ἐλέπτολις ἐκ τῶν

| Anacreontic | Link | Ionic a minore |

ἀβροτίμων προκαλυμμάτων ἔπλευσεν Ζεφύρου γίγαντος αὔρᾳ . . .

| Ionic a m. | Anacreontic |

Bacchylides, addressing Theseus, 'King of the delicately-living Ionians,' gives us a suggestion of the same rhythm:

Bacchyl. xvii 1–2

Βασιλεῦ τᾶν ἱερᾶν Ἀθανᾶν, τῶν ἀβροβίων ἄναξ Ἰώνων.

Stesichorus, who sang of the martial exploits of the Greeks in Dorian rhythm, sang of the loves of Leontichus and Rhadine of Samos in Ionic a minore:

Stesich. 44

ἄγε, Μοῦσα λίγει', ἄρξον ἀοιδᾶς ἐρατωνύμου

Σαμίων περὶ παίδων ἐρατᾷ φθεγγομένα λύρᾳ.

—FOR
IONIA
AND ASIA

Just as Dorian rhythm was extended beyond its primary association with the Dorians so as to embrace the Greeks as a whole, so Ionic a minore came to be used of the inhabitants of Asia generally, barbarian as well as Ionian. In the *Persae*, it accompanies the description of the manhood of Asia which has gone forth to meet the Greeks at Salamis:

Aesch. *Pers.* 66–116

πεπέρακεν μὲν ὁ περσέπτολις ἤδη βασίλειος στρατὸς εἰς ἀντίπορον γείτονα χώραν . . .

Pindar uses it with similar effect in the seventh Olympian[1]. Diagoras, whose victory he celebrates, comes from the Dorian city of Rhodes. But Rhodes, before its colonization by the Dorians, was Ionian; and in delicate allusion to this mixed origin of the Rhodians Pindar softens his Dorian rhythm, in which the main part of the poem is composed, with a few light touches of Ionic a minore:

[1] Headlam, *J. H. S.* vol. XXII, pp. 224–6.

Pind. *O*. vii

(1) Φιάλαν ὡς εἴ τις ἀφνεᾶς ἀπὸ χειρὸς ἑλών
<u>Ionic a m.</u>　<u>Dorian</u>

(6) παρεόντων θῆκέ νιν ζαλωτὸν ὁμόφρονος εὐνᾶς
<u>Ionic a m.</u>　<u>Dorian</u>

　　　<u>Dorian</u>
(18) Ἀσίας εὐρυχόρου τρίπολιν νᾶσον πέλας
<u>Ionic a m.</u>

Lastly, we may observe that Ionic a minore is one of the —FOR
leading motives in the *Bacchae*. That is because the hero of DIONYSUS
that play, Dionysus, was not in origin a Greek god. He was
a newcomer to Olympus; and he came out of Asia[1].

Eur. *Bacch*. 64–5[2]

Ἀσίας ἀπὸ γαίας ἱερὸν Τμῶλον ἀμείψασα θοάζω . . .

Ibid. 83–88

ἴτε βάκχαι, ἴτε βάκχαι, Βρόμιον παῖδα θεὸν θεοῦ
Διόνυσον κατάγουσαι Φρυγίων ἐξ ὀρέων Ἑλ-
　　<u>Pherecratic</u>　　<u>Choriambus</u>
λάδος εὐρυχόρους ἀγυιάς, τὸν Βρόμιον.

Similar to Ionic a minore in form, though different in effect, CHOR-
is choriambic. It is a rapid, lively measure suitable to restless IAMBIC
or animated motion. Aeschylus uses it in *The Suppliants* for
the flight of the vanquished, and for the wanderings of Io[3];
Sophocles, for the turmoil of battle:

Soph. *Ant*. 138–40
　　　　　　　　　　　　　　　<u>Pherecratic</u>
ἄλλα δ' ἐπ' ἄλλοις ἐπενώμα στυφελίζων μέγας Ἄρης δεξιόσειρος.
<u>Choriambic</u>

---

[1] Ionic a minore is again used for Dionysus in Ar. *Ran*. 324–36.

[2] 64 I read γαίας for γᾶς : cf. 68 τίς ὁδῷ, τίς ὁδῷ, τίς;

[3] See below Chap. VIII; and cf. Ar. *Lys*. 321–49. There was nothing particularly
solemn about it (J. M. Edmonds, *Lyra Graeca*, III, p. 589 note).

Euripides uses it for the flight of Perseus:

Eur. *El.* 458–63

περιδρόμῳ μὲν ἴτυος ἕδρᾳ
Glyconic (resolved)
Περσέα λαιμοτόμαν ὑπὲρ
Enneasyllable
Iambo-choriambic   Glyconic . . .
ἁλὸς ποτανοῖσι πεδίλοισι φύαν Γοργόνος ἴσχειν, Διὸς ἀγ-
            Choriambic
(contd.)   Pherecratic
γέλῳ σὺν Ἑρμᾷ, τῷ Μαίας ἀγροτῆρι κούρῳ.
            Choriambic

And for the lioness in chase of her prey:

Ibid. 471–5 (same rhythm)

ἐπὶ δὲ χρυσοτύπῳ κράνει
Σφίγγες ὄνυξιν ἀοίδιμον
ἄγραν φέρουσαι· περιπλεύρῳ δὲ κύτει πύρπνοος ἔσπευδε δρόμῳ
λέαινα χαλαῖς Πειρηναῖον ὁρῶσα πῶλον.

Simonides for the winter storms:

Simon. 12[1]

ὡς ὁπόταν χειμέριον κατὰ μῆνα πινύσκῃ
Ζεὺς ἄματα τέσσαρα καὶ δέκα . . .

Sometimes it denotes mental rather than physical agitation:

Aesch. *Cho.* 390–2

πάροιθεν δὲ πρῴρας δριμὺς ἄηται κραδίας θυμός, ἔγκοτον στύγος.

CHOR-   And hence it comes to be associated with the inspired frenzy
IAMBIC   of the *prophet*:
FOR
PROPHECY   Soph. *O. T.* 483–4

δεινὰ μὲν οὖν δεινὰ ταράσσει σοφὸς οἰωνοθέτας . . .

Aesch. *Supp.* 58

εἰ δὲ κυρεῖ τις πέλας οἰωνοπολῶν . . .

[1] Cf. Soph. *O. C.* 1240–1 βόρειος ὥς τις ἀκτὰ κυματόπληξ χειμερία κλονεῖται.

Aesch. *Agam.* 208–12

ἐπεὶ δὲ καὶ πικροῦ χείματος ἄλλο μῆχαρ βριθύτερον πρόμοισιν
Iambic ――――――――――――――――― Pherecratic ――――――― Pherecratic

μάντις ἔκλαγξεν προφέρων Ἄρτεμιν, ὥστε . . .
Choriambic

Soph. *El.* 473–4

Aeolian tripody

εἰ μὴ 'γὼ παράφρων μάντις ἔφυν καὶ γνώμας λειπομένα σοφᾶς . .

Soph. *O.T.* 1086–8

εἴπερ ἐγὼ μάντις εἰμὶ καὶ κατὰ γνώμαν ἴδρις,

οὐ τὸν Ὄλυμπον ἀπείρων . . .

In the last example the metre is pure Dorian ; but the initial prosodiac suggests choriambic.

Mid-way between these Ionian rhythms and Dorian comes AEOLIAN Aeolian : it is neither solemn like Dorian, nor so relaxed and passionate as Ionian. In general, its effect may be said to be light and tender. Like Ionic a minore, it is used for lamentation, but for a grief less abandoned, more pensive and pathetic.

Aesch. *Agam.* 1449–50

φεῦ, τίς ἂν ἐν τάχει, μὴ περιώδυνος, μηδὲ δεμνιοτήρης . . .

This is the first time we have heard Aeolian since the murder of Agamemnon ; and coming, as it does, after the impassioned Paeonic of the long Cassandra scene, it serves to relieve the emotional tension. It appears again at the opening of the invocation in the *Choephoroe*:

Aesch. *Cho.* 314–17[1]

ὦ πάτερ αἰνόπατερ, τί σοι φάμενος ἢ τί ῥέξας,

τύχοιμ' ἂν τόθεν οὐρίσας, ἔνθα σ' ἔχουσιν εὐναί;

We hear it again at the end of the same scene, when the

――――――

[1] τόθεν or σ' ἔκαθ' Headlam : ἔκαθεν.

Chorus, exhausted by their passionate appeal for vengeance, turn once more to lamentation:

Aesch. *Cho.* 464-6

ὦ πόνος ἐγγενὴς καὶ παράμουσος ἄτης αἱματόεσσα πλαγά.

It has a similar effect in the *Electra* of Sophocles:

Soph. *El.* 245-6

εἰ γὰρ ὁ μὲν θανὼν γᾶ τε καὶ οὐδὲν ὢν κείσεται τάλας.

Trochaic

Soph. *O. T.* 1186-1204

ἰὼ γενεαὶ βροτῶν, ὡς ὑμᾶς ἴσα καὶ τὸ μηδὲν ζώσας ἐναριθμῶ.

Soph. *Phil.* 169-90

οἰκτίρω νιν ἔγωγ᾽ ὅπως μή του κηδομένου βροτῶν

μηδὲ ξύντροφον ὄμμ᾽ ἔχων, δύστανος, μόνος αἰεί, . . .

Soph. *O. C.* 1211-38

μὴ φῦναι τὸν ἅπαντα νικᾷ λόγον· τὸ δ᾽, ἐπεὶ φανῇ,

βῆναι κεῖσ᾽ ὁπόθεν περ ἥκει πολὺ δεύτερον ὡς τάχιστα.

But Aeolian is not invariably set to sorrowful themes. So long as the poetical tone is light and tender, Aeolian provides an appropriate accompaniment. It is often found in conjunction with merrymaking, singing and dancing. It is in Aeolian that the Suppliants pray the gods to shower all manner of blessings on the city which has undertaken to protect them:

Aesch. *Supp.* 702-5

εὐφήμοις δ᾽ ἐπὶ βωμοῖς μοῦσαν θείατ᾽ ἀοιδοί·

ἁγνῶν τ᾽ ἐκ στομάτων φερέσθω φήμα φιλοφόρμιγξ.

Eur. *H.F.* 348-51

αἴλινον μὲν ἐπ᾽ εὐτυχεῖ μολπᾷ Φοῖβος ἰαχεῖ

τὸν κάλλει φθιτόν, κιθάραν ἐλαύνων πλήκτρῳ χρυσέῳ.

The Thebans rejoice over the deliverance of their city from the villainous Lynceus in this measure:

Ibid. 763–4[1]

χοροὶ χοροὶ καὶ θαλίαι μέλουσι Θήβας ἱερὸν κατ᾽ ἄστυ.

The Bacchants long for their midnight dances:

Eur. *Bacch.* 862–96

ἆρ᾽ ἐν παννυχίοις χοροῖς θήσω ποτὲ λευκὸν
πόδ᾽ ἀναβακχεύουσα, δέραν εἰς αἰθέρα δροσερὸν ῥίπτουσ᾽
                     Protracted Pherecratic[2]
ὡς νεβρὸς χλοεραῖς ἐμπαίζουσα λείμακος ἡδοναῖς . . .
Protracted Pherecratic

The captive Trojans look back on the days when the sounds of revelry were heard in the city:

Eur. *Tro.* 1071–6

φροῦδαί σοι θυσίαι χορῶν τ᾽ εὔφημοι κέλαδοι κατ᾽ ὄρ-
φναν τε παννυχίδες θεῶν, χρυσέων τε ξοάνων τύποι
Φρυγῶν τε ζάθεοι σελᾶναι συνδώδεκα πλήθει.

Anacreon, the poet of wine and song, makes frequent use of Aeolian:

Anacr. 17

ἠρίστησα μὲν ἰτρίου λεπτοῦ μικρὸν ἀποκλάς,
οἴνου δ᾽ ἐξέπιον κάδον, νῦν δ᾽ ἀβρῶς ἐρόεσσαν
ψάλλω πηκτίδα τῇ φίλῃ κωμάζων †παιδὶ ἁβρῇ.†

Sometimes he combines it with the more lively choriambic:

Anacr. 24
            Pherecratic
ἀναπέτομαι δὴ πρὸς Ὄλυμπον πτερύγεσσι κούφαις
Choriambic
            Pherecratic
διὰ τὸν Ἔρωτ᾽· οὐ γὰρ ἐμοὶ παῖς ἐθέλει συνηβᾶν.
Choriambic

CHOR-
IAMBIC
AND
AEOLIAN
COMBINED

---

[1] Cf. 781–9, a reminiscence of Soph. *Ant.* 100–9, in the same rhythm.

[2] The analysis is: ⌐‑ ⌣⌣⌣ ⌐‑⌐ for ⌐‑ ⌣⌣ ⌐‑‑.

The fashion set by Anacreon was followed by many a nameless author of drinking-songs:

Scolium 22, Bergk III, p. 650

σύν μοι πῖνε, συνήβα, συνέρα, συστεφανηφόρει,
σύν μοι μαινομένῳ μαίνεο, σὺν σώφρονι σωφρόνει.

Hence when Euripides sings of Anacreon's favourite theme —the delights of fleeting youth, the cares of approaching age —he uses the rhythm which Anacreon has made familiar:

Eur. *H.F.* 637–41

Pherecratic
ἁ νεότας μοι φίλον αἰεί· τὸ δὲ γῆρας ἄχθος
Choriambic

Pherecratic
βαρύτερον Αἴτνας σκοπέλων ἐπὶ κρατὶ κεῖται βλεφάρων σκο-
Choriambic   Pherecratic . . .

Pherecratic
τεινὸν φάος ἐπικάλυψαν.
(*contd.*)

Weary of war, the Trojans sing:

Eur. *Rh.* 360–7

Glyconic   Glyconic
ἀρά ποτ' αὖθις ἁ παλαιὰ Τροία τοὺς προπότας παναμερεύ-
      Iambo-choriambic   Anacreontic

Pherecratic
σει θιάσους ἐρώτων

               Choriambic
ψαλμοῖσι καὶ κυλίκων οἰνοπλανήτων ὑποδεξίαις ἀμίλ-
Epitrite   Anacreontic
Dorian

λαις κατὰ πόντον Ἀτρειδᾶν Σπάρταν οἰχομένων
      Pherecratic
      Ἰλιάδος παρ' ἀκτᾶς;

Will the city of Troy ever again ring to the sounds of night-long merrymaking? They are heard in the rhythm. Will the Greeks ever cease from fighting? We hear for a moment the sturdy Dorian; and then, as—in the singer's imagination—

the invaders retreat across the sea, leaving Troy in peace, the Dorian rhythm dies away, and we return to Aeolian[1].

Dorian for the Dorians, Ionic a minore for the Ionians. It would be strange if the Athenian poets failed to select a rhythm which would be as appropriate to Athens as Dorian to her Peloponnesian rivals and Ionian to the cities beyond the Aegean. Their choice fell on the brilliant rhythm which occupied an intermediate place between the two—Aeolian. The sailors of Salamis muse with longing over the glories of their island home:

AEOLIAN FOR ATHENS

Soph. *Aj.* 596–9

ὦ κλεινὰ Σάλαμις, σὺ μέν που ναίεις ἁλίπλακτος εὐδαί-
μων πᾶσιν περίφαντος αἰεί.

They yearn for the sight of the Athenian acropolis, which greets the eyes of the homecoming seafarer as he rounds Cape Sunium:

Ibid. 1217–22

γενοίμαν ἵν' ὑλᾶεν ἔπεστι πόντου πρόβλημ' ἁλικλύστον, ἄ-
Bacchius Anac. Glyconic   Glyconic

                         Anacl. Pherecratic
κραν ὑπὸ πλάκα Σουνίου, τὰς ἱερὰς ὅπως προσείποιμεν Ἀθάνας.
Glyconic   Glyconic

The Argive Herald threatens war if the Athenians refuse to give up Heracles' widow and children. They reply that theirs is a city not accustomed to yield to menaces:

Eur. *Hcld.* 358–61

μήπω ταῖς μεγάλαισιν οὕτω καὶ καλλιχόροις Ἀθή-
ναις εἴη· σὺ δ' ἄφρων, ὅ τ' Ἄργει Σθενέλου τύραννος.

And, after the victory has been won, they rejoice that their city has granted to the children of Heracles the protection which their guardian-goddess Athena gave to Heracles himself:

---

[1] Thus the scheme of this passage is similar to that of Eur. *I. A.* 751-5 (see above, p. 49).

Ibid. 919–23

συμφέρεται τὰ πολλὰ πολλοῖς· καὶ γὰρ πατρὶ τῶνδ' 'Αθάναν

λέγουσ' ἐπίκουρον εἶναι, καὶ τούσδε θεᾶς πόλις καὶ λαὸς ἔσωσε

κείνας.

Aristophanes varies his Aeolian with a touch of Anacreontic:

Ar. *Eq.* 581–94[1]

Anacreontic

ὦ πολιοῦχε Παλλάς, ὦ τῆς ἱερωτάτης ἀπα-

(A) Aeolian

σῶν πολέμῳ τε καὶ ποιηταῖς δυνάμει θ' ὑπερφερού-

σης μεδέουσα χώρας,

δεῦρ' ἀφικοῦ λαβοῦσα τὴν ἐν στρατιαῖς τε καὶ μάχαις

ἡμέτερον ξυνεργὸν

Νίκην, ἣ χορικῶν ἐστιν ἑταίρα, τοῖς τ' ἐχθροῖσι μεθ' ἡ-

(B) Dorian

μῶν στασιάζει.

νῦν οὖν δεῦρο φάνηθι· δεῖ γὰρ τοῖς ἀνδράσι τοῖσδε πά-

(A) Aeolian

σῃ τέχνῃ πορίσαι σε νίκην εἴπερ ποτὲ καὶ νῦν.

The Knights call upon Athena in Aeolian; but, at the name Νίκη, as they pray for victory in battle, the rhythm changes and we hear a touch of Dorian. Is this an accident? Anyhow, Niké dwells with Zeus in Olympus:

Bacchyl. x. 1 (Dorian)

Νίκα [γλυκύδωρε, μεγίσταν σοὶ πα]τὴρ ὤπασσε τιμὰν

ὑψίζυγ[ος Οὐρανιδᾶν] ἐν πολυχρύσῳ δ' 'Ολύμπῳ

Ζηνὶ παρισταμένα.

The famous ode in the *Oedipus Coloneus* begins:

Soph. *O. C.* 668–719

Anacreontic

εὐίππου, ξένε, τᾶσδε χώρας ἵκου τὰ κράτιστα γᾶς ἔπαυλα.

Glyconic   Glyconic

This is common Aeolian, passing into Anacreontic, as in the

---

[1] Aeolian is again used for Athena in Ar. *Thesm.* 1137–47.

previous example. The poet then returns to Aeolian to describe the song of the nightingale as he has often heard it in his native woods at Colonus. In his second strophe he goes on to describe the greatest glory of the Athenian country-side—the olive:

Pherecratic	Ionic a minore
ἔστιν δ' οἷον ἐγὼ γᾶς	'Ασίας οὐκ ἐπακούω,

echo[1]

Dorian	Ionic a minore
οὐδ' ἐν τᾷ μεγάλᾳ Δωρίδι νάσῳ	Πέλοπος πώποτε βλαστὸν

Dochmiac	Trochaic
φύτευμ' ἀχείρωτον αὐτόποιον	ἐγχέων φόβημα δαΐων,

Dochmiac

ὃ τᾷδε θάλλει μέγιστα χώρᾳ,

Dorian

γλαυκᾶς παιδοτρόφου φύλλον ἐλαίας·

Dochmiac[2]

τὸ μέν τις οὐ νεαρὸς οὐδὲ γήρᾳ

Ionic a minore	Glyconic[3]
συνναίων ἁλιώσει χερὶ πέρσας·	ὁ γὰρ εἰσαιὲν ὁρῶν κύκλος

echo

Glyconic	Pherecratic
λεύσσει νιν Μορίου Διὸς	χά γλαυκῶπις 'Αθάνα.

That this design is woven out of diverse rhythms is plain enough. But observe how it is made to enforce the significance of the poetry. There is a plant which does not grow on Asiatic soil ('Ασίας οὐκ ἐπακούω)—the rhythm is Ionic a minore ; nor in the Dorian isle of Pelops (οὐδ' ἐν τᾷ μεγάλᾳ Δωρίδι νάσῳ)[4]

[1] For this shift, cf. Aesch. Supp. 60-1 (p. 27).

[2] ⌣⌣⌣⌣|⌣⌣⌣: cf. Aesch. Theb. 508 πέποιθα τὸν Διός.

[3] This is the Euripidean Glyconic that arouses the indignation of Aeschylus in the Frogs (1320-3) οἰνάνθας γάνος ἀμπέλου, βότρυος ἕλικα παυσίπονον. περίβαλλ' ὦ τέκνον ὠλένας, i.e. ⌣⌣_ ⌣⌣ ⌣⌣ ⌣ for _⌣_ ⌣⌣ ⌣⌣ ⌣. Sophocles, however, might plead the excuse that, as he uses it, it provides a pretty transition from Ionic a minore.

[4] I am aware that, taken syllable by syllable, this phrase might be regarded as Ionic a minore, like the last: but the natural rhythm of the words, to my ear, is unmistakably prosodiac.

—the rhythm is Dorian: but only in Attica, where it shall never perish, for it flourishes under the watchful eyes of Zeus and Pallas Athena (λεύσσει νιν Μορίου Διὸς χά γλαυκῶπις Ἀθάνα)—the rhythm is Aeolian. Rarely have words and rhythm been wedded in so perfect a harmony[1].

PAEONIC —FOR CRETE   One other class of rhythm remains to be discussed—Paeonic. If Dorian was proper to the Dorians, Ionic a minore to the Ionians, Aeolian to Athens, Paeonic seems to have had a special connexion with Crete.

Simon. 31

ὅταν δὲ γηρῶσαι . . . ἐλαφρὸν ὄρχημ᾽ ἀοιδᾶ ποδῶν μιγνύμεν·
Κρῆτά μιν καλέοισι τρόπον, τό θ᾽ ὄργανον Μολοσσόν.
Aeolian

Mel. fr. adesp. 118

Κρησίοις ἐν ῥυθμοῖς παῖδα μέλψωμεν . . .

Ar. *Ran.* 1356–7

ἀλλ᾽, ὦ Κρῆτες, Ἴδας τέκνα, τὰ τόξα λαβόντες ἐπαμύνατε.

Bacchylides uses Paeonic for his sixteenth ode—the story of Theseus' expedition to Crete. Apollo, too, according to an ancient tradition, came from Crete: hence we find that Paeonic, as well as Dorian, is used for that god.

Simon. 26 B

—FOR APOLLO AND ARTEMIS   Δαλογενές, εἴτε Λυκίαν . . . χρυσεοκόμας Ἕκατε, παῖ Διός.

Aesch. *Agam.* 1064–5

Ἄπολλον Ἄπολλον ἀγυιᾶτ᾽ Ἀπόλλων ἐμός.

Ibid. 153[2]

ἰήϊον δὲ καλέω Παιᾶνα.

---

[1] For other examples of Aeolian for Athens, cf. Eur. *Hcld.* 748–54, *Ion* 184–9.
[2] The third foot (Παιᾶνα) is a παλιμβάκχειος: see Appendix. Alcman used Paeonic for his hymn to Apollo's sister, Artemis: 19 οὐδὲ τῶ Κνακάλω οὐδὲ τῶ Νυρσύλα.

Soph. *Trach.* 205–24

<u>ἀνολολυξάτω δόμος ἐφεστίοις ἀλαλαγαῖς</u>

<u>ὁ μελλόνυμφος· ἐν δὲ κοινὸς ἀρσένων</u>
Iambic trimeter
<u>ἴτω κλαγγὰ τὸν εὐφαρέτραν Ἀπόλλωνα προστάταν.</u>

Mel. fr. adesp. 85

<u>ὕμνον ὧν κλύετε· πέμπω δέ νιν</u>

<u>ὡς σέ, Κλειθέμιος παῖ,</u>
Aeolian
Aeolian
<u>Ἀπόλλωνι μὲν θεῶν, ἀτὰρ ἀνδρῶν Ἐχεκράτει παιδὶ Πυθαγγέλω.</u>

The principal function of Paeonic rhythm, apart from these —FOR EX-
particular associations, was to accompany intense or violent CITEMENT
emotion, such as terror or religious fervour[1]. In this capacity
it was much used by the dramatists, and will be considered
when we come to discuss how the dramatists used all these
rhythms, not merely for the sake of passing effects, but as
part of the very fibre of their plots.

The Dorian mode, as we saw at the beginning of this
chapter, was Greek, the Ionian un-Greek, in effect. The
Dorian was ἀνδρώδης, μεγαλοπρεπής[2], σεμνός[3], μέτριος, σώ-
φρων[4]: the Ionian γλαφυρός[5], μαλακός, συμποτικός[6]. The
Mixolydian was θρηνώδης[7], the Phrygian ἔνθεος[8]. Without
attempting to identify mode with rhythm too closely, we are
now in a position to point out that these are the very attri-
butes we should ascribe to the different rhythms in view of
the emotional quality of the poetry which they accompany.
It is clear therefore that the distinction between one rhythm

---

[1] Cretics, in particular, are used for earnest entreaty: Aesch. *Supp.* 423–8 φρόντισον καὶ γενοῦ κτλ. (see below, p. 91), Soph. *O. T.* 649–53 πιθοῦ θελήσας φρονήσας
τ', ἄναξ, λίσσομαι, Ar. *Eccl.* 952 f. δεῦρο δὴ δεῦρο δή, φίλον ἐμόν, δεῦρό μοι πρόσελθε
καὶ ξύνευνος τὴν εὐφρόνην ὅπως ἔσει (an amusing piece of musical parody).

[2] Athen. xiv, 624. [3] Plut. *de Mus.* xvii. [4] Plat. *Rep.* iii, 399 A.
[5] Lucian, *Harmon.* 1. [6] Plat. *ibid.* 398 E. [7] *Ibid.* 398 E.
[8] Lucian, *ibid.* 1.

and another, as between one mode and another, was partly ethical. And in the case of rhythm we may go further and say that the poets took advantage of these ethical distinctions to evolve an elaborate convention of significant music. How elaborate the convention was, we cannot say, because the melodies, which presumably enforced the significance of the words as emphatically as the rhythms, have perished. But we know that few peoples have had sharper ears than the Greeks, or a keener sense of poetry. We need not be surprised therefore, if the Greek poet, relying on the quickness of his audience, sometimes invested his rhythms with a significance even more subtle than those I have explained above. We remember that charming fragment of Simonides, in which poor Danae, adrift on the waves of the sea, lulls her child to sleep.

Simon. 37. 9–19

Dorian
ἄλμαν δ' ὕπερθεν τεᾶν κομᾶν βαθεῖαν

Ionic a m.   Dorian
παριόντος κύματος οὐκ ἀλέγεις, οὐδ' ἀνέμων φθόγγον, πορφυρέᾳ
a   b   b   b

κείμενος ἐν χλανίδι, πρόσωπον κλιθὲν προσώπῳ.
c

                Aeolian tripody   Echoes[1]
εἰ δέ τοι δεινὸν τό γε δεινὸν ἦν, καί κεν ἐμῶν ῥημάτων
                    d   from b   from d
Pherecratic, from c
λεπτὸν ὑπεῖχες οὖας.

Echo from a   Anacreontic
κέλομαι δ' εὖδε, βρέφος, εὑδέτω δὲ πόντος,

Glyconic   Anacreontic
εὑδέτω δ' ἄμοτον κακόν· μεταιβολία δέ τις φανείη,
                        echo

[1] ⏑‿‿⏑ ⏑‿⏑ : this phrase grows naturally out of a Glyconic or Aeolian tripody: cf. Pind. P. x, 2 μάκαιρα Θεσσαλία· πατρὸς δ' ἀμφοτέραις ἐξ ἑνός: and cf. H. D. F. Kitto, C. R. XLII, pp. 51–3.

Dorian

Ζεῦ πάτερ, ἐκ σέθεν· ὅττι δὲ θαρσαλέον ἔπος εὔχομαι νόσ-
φιν δίκας, σύγγνωθί μοι.

The rhythm has passed from Dorian, through Aeolian, into Anacreontic, and finally, at the mention of the name of Zeus, back to Dorian. The effect of those Anacreontics, in conjunction with Aeolian and in contrast to Dorian, is tender, pathetic; and that in itself would be sufficient reason for introducing them. At the same time, I cannot help thinking that Simonides had in mind, and wished to recall to his audience, a poem of Alcman's:

Alcm. 60

εὕδουσιν δ' ὀρέων κορυφαί τε καὶ φάραγγες,
Dorian   Anacreontic

πρώονές τε καὶ χαράδραι,
Dorian

φύλλα θ' ἑρπετά θ' ὅσσα τρέφει μέλαινα γαῖα,
Aeolian tripody   Anacreontic

θῆρές τ' ὀρεσκῷοι καὶ γένος μελισσᾶν
Dorian[1]

καὶ κνώδαλ' ἐν βένθεσι πορφυρέας ἁλός·
        Glyconic

εὕδουσιν δ' οἰωνῶν φῦλα τανυπτερύγων.
Dorian

Here too the principal subject is Dorian, and here again it is blended—to my ear very happily—with Aeolian and Anacreontic. The Greek poets collaborated in a conscious striving, not after novelty, but after an artistic ideal, and each successive artist knew that his own work would gain, not lose, by being displayed against the background provided by the work of his predecessors. As Bacchylides well said:

ἕτερος ἐξ ἑτέρου σοφὸς τό τε πάλαι τό τε νῦν.

---

[1] The first of these epitrites is a good example of *rallentando* effect obtained by anacrusis and protraction.

CHAPTER SEVEN

PINDAR'S FIRST OLYMPIAN

THE modern reader, making the acquaintance of the Odes of Pindar for the first time, is apt to be puzzled by their apparent incoherence. He admires the fine language, the swiftness and the wealth of splendid imagery, but he is bewildered by the abrupt changes of subject and the seeming lack of any close unity of form. He feels perhaps that the lines of Horace, intended as praise of the poet's style, might be equally justified as a criticism of the arrangement of his subject-matter:

> monte decurrens velut amnis, imbres
> quem super notas aluere ripas,
> fervet immensusque ruit profundo
> Pindarus ore.

Does the fault lie with the poet or with his reader? The novice in modern music, as he listens to one of Beethoven's symphonies for the first time, feels similarly at a loss. He is impressed by many fine and moving passages, and receives at the end, perhaps, a sense of satisfaction and finality, but he is a little puzzled all the same. As his acquaintance with the symphony advances, this difficulty resolves itself: he comes to feel that, so far from being chaotic, it is really an organic unity, in which each part performs a definite function in relation to the whole. And if he pursues his enquiry still further, he will find that the musician is directing his inspiration along certain well-recognised channels of musical form. The work of Pindar is entitled to the same consideration. Modern literary critics devote less attention than musical critics to artistic form—in modern poetry it is less important. But in Greek poetry—related so closely, as we have seen, to music—it is essential. This is the key to the solution of our difficulty in understanding Pindar.

The First Olympian celebrates the victory of Hiero of Syracuse, and his horse Pherenicus, at the festival of 476. In order to understand the poem, it will help us if we try to envisage the circumstances in which it was performed. The banquet is over, Hiero and his guests recline on their couches, drinking the wine with which their golden cups are replenished by the beautiful pages in attendance on the feast. The musicians and the dancers come in, room is made for them in the body of the hall, and the ode begins—a blend of song and dance, in which the poet tells of the love of Poseidon for Pelops, son of Tantalus—how he carried him off to Olympus to serve, like Ganymede, at the banquets of the Immortals. According to the old story, the gods feasted on his flesh. But that was a lie: the gods are not cannibals. No, Poseidon stole Pelops for love. Even so, however, he was not to enjoy his company in heaven for long. The boy's father, Tantalus, upon whom the gods had bestowed the gift of immortality, grew over-proud in his prosperity, and stole from them their nectar and ambrosia. For this sin he was cast into Hades, and his son sent back to the life on earth, where, with the help of his heavenly lover, he overthrew the King of Elis, made the King's daughter his bride, and the glorious festival of Olympia was founded in his honour.

The poet begins with praise of the festival, "like water, or gold, or the sun in the sky." The names of Zeus, the god of Olympia, and of Hiero, the victor, are coupled together, and with them a suggestion of the poet himself, by whose art the greatness of both is fitly celebrated. In the middle of the ode comes the myth—the story of Poseidon's love for Pelops. Finally, the poet completes his design by reminding us of the themes with which the ode began. We have just heard how Pelops was accorded, at the end of his days, an honoured burial in Olympia: and this brings us back to the thought of the Olympian festival, Hiero's victory. May God, who watches over him, grant him in the time to come a yet more splendid victory—in the chariot-race! Kings are the greatest of men:

only, let them not peer too far—let not their greatness beget
in them the pride that ruined Tantalus! And, in the mean-
time, the greatest of kings shall continue to be honoured by
the greatest of poets.

A   The Olympian Festival.
    Zeus, poets, Hiero.
       The victory of Pherenicus.

B   Poseidon's love for Pelops.
          False legends.
       Poseidon's love for Pelops.
          False legends.
            Tantalus ruined by pride in prosperity.
       Poseidon's love for Pelops: the race with Oenomaus.

A   The Olympian Festival.
       The victory of Pherenicus.
    God, Hiero—
          Moderation in prosperity.
    The poet.

It would be a pleasant task to examine other odes of Pindar,
and show how they, too, are designed in similar fashion; to
compare the lyric technique of Pindar with the dramatic technique of Aeschylus, and to trace both back to their common
origin in the epic technique of Homer. But that would lead
us beyond the scope of this book: we must content ourselves
with observing that here we have an excellent illustration of
the use, for the purposes of poetry, of those principles of formal
composition which we have already examined in relation to
rhythm.

Let us now look at the metre of the poem, and see how it
contributes to the general effect. First of all, we must analyse
the metrical form; and to do that, we turn to the first strophe,
in obedience to a principle which Pindar observes in all his
odes. As was said in the first chapter, the surest means of
discovering the metre of a piece of Greek lyric is to read it

according to the sense of the words, which the metre is designed to emphasise. Pindar begins his odes by stating the metrical form in the clearest manner possible—that is, by making the rhythmical periods and the sense-periods coincide. But as the poem proceeds, as strophe is followed by antistrophe and epode by epode, the metrical form becomes increasingly familiar to the ear; and so, without danger of obscurity, the poet can vary his design by making his sense-periods run counter to the periods dictated by the metrical form, by introducing pauses in the sense in the middle of a phrase, or by allowing the words to run over from one phrase into another. By this means what might have been crude and stereotyped, becomes subtle and capable of infinite variety[1].

Let us begin, then, with the first sentence:

Ἄριστον μὲν ὕδωρ, ὁ δὲ χρυσὸς αἰθόμενον πῦρ

ἅτε διαπρέπει νυκτὶ μεγάνορος ἔξοχα πλούτου.

That is plain enough. First of all, we have a Glyconic followed by a Pherecratic—a combination already familiar to us under the name of the Aeolian couplet. Pindar begins his poem by stating in the simplest terms this very simple rhythm. The only peculiarity to be noticed is that the opening of the Glyconic is inverted—that is to say, it is anaclastic—a variant so common that Pindar can trust his audience to recognise it at once. Next comes a short figure: ◡◡◡⏌◡⏌. The falling rhythm of the preceding Pherecratic inclines us to take it as trochaic—as a resolved form of ⏌◡⏌◡⏌. And the last figure confirms this impression: it is in strongly-marked falling rhythm—a prosodiac.

εἰ δ' ἄεθλα γαρύεν ἔλδεαι, φίλον ἦτορ, μηκέθ' ἀλίου σκόπει

ἄλλο θαλπνότερον ἐν ἀμέρᾳ φαεννὸν ἄστρον ἐρημᾶς δι' αἰθέρος,

This is rather more elaborate. First we return to trochaic—a

---

[1] See Headlam, *J.H.S.* vol. XXII, p. 216. And compare, in this ode, the first strophe with the third or the fourth antistrophe.

dimeter this time, and that in turn is followed by another Pherecratic; then a dimeter again. The opening of the next phrase, also, is clearly trochaic—a trimeter with the third foot resolved: but it passes, by overlap of one syllable, into yet a third Pherecratic. Previously we heard the trochaic and Pherecratic movements separately; now they are dovetailed together. And what of that figure at the end of the last phrase—δι᾽ αἰθέρος? It seems to be iambic, in rising rhythm, thus carrying on the hints of rising rhythm already let fall in ἄριστον and in ἅτε διαπρέπει. Let us proceed.

μηδ᾽ Ὀλυμπίας ἀγῶνα φέρτερον αὐδάσομεν·

Again the opening is trochaic (a dimeter); again the trochaic passes by overlap of one syllable into a Pherecratic; and again the Pherecratic is followed by an iambic appendage—shorter this time, and not marked off, as before, by the division of the words.

We have now come to the end of the second musical sentence, and we notice how both have been marked off by the two pauses in the sense. Looking back over this, the first rhythmical period, we find that falling rhythm has prevailed— Aeolian and trochaic, with a diversion into dactylic: but at the same time we have heard suggestions of rising rhythm which make us await with interest the second period, to see whether those suggestions will be followed up.

ὅθεν ὁ πολύφατος ὕμνος ἀμφιβάλλεται

We have already come across this phrase as a beautiful example of shift by resolution[1]. The two opening feet are tribrachs, of which the first suggests trochaic, while the second is neutral, and so brings us to plain iambic. By this means the transition to rising rhythm is completed.

Pindar has still one more development in store for us before bringing his strophe to a close. Iambic suggests another rising

---

[1] See above, p. 24.

rhythm—Paeonic. And that is why he has introduced iambic here:

σοφῶν μητίεσσι, κελαδεῖν Κρόνου παῖδ' ἐς ἀφνεὰν ἱκομένους
μάκαιραν Ἱέρωνος ἑστίαν.

Iambic has given place to Paeonic. And now we see why the initial Glyconic was anaclastic—ἄριστον suggests a bacchius (σοφῶν μη- Κρόνου παῖδ'); and why the first foot of that trochaic figure ἅτε διαπρέπει was resolved—it may be regarded equally well as a dochmiac.

Thus, starting from Aeolian, the poet has led us through trochaic and iambic to Paeonic, and he has worked his transitions with such skill that each step follows smoothly and naturally from the last.

Now turn to the epode. The strophe has led us from Aeolian through trochaic and iambic to Paeonic. The epode will lead us back again.

Συρακόσιον ἱπποχάρμαν βασιλῆα· λάμπει δέ οἱ κλέος

There is no difficulty here: first, dochmiac; then a Pherecratic; and the Pherecratic is again followed by that iambic appendage with which the strophe has made us familiar.

ἐν εὐάνορι Λυδοῦ Πέλοπος ἀποικίᾳ.

The first of these figures is new—or rather an old figure under a new disguise. It is a Pherecratic with anaclasis: ◡⏒–◡◡ ⏒– instead of ⏒◡ ⏒◡◡ ⏒–. The opening ἐν εὐά- suggests a bacchius, like ἄριστον at the beginning of the strophe; and if the first half of the figure echoes Paeonic, the second (νορι Λυδοῦ) adds a touch—transitory and slight—of Ionic a minore. Then we have another iambic figure, with the first foot resolved. Why? The resolution (Πέλοπος) prepares us for the next figure—trochaic:

τοῦ μεγασθενὴς ἐράσσατο γαιάοχος

This phrase reminds us of one already heard in the strophe:

μηδ' 'Ολυμπίας ἀγῶνα φέρτερον αὐδάσομεν.

It is, in fact, identical, except that this time the poet, relying on our familiarity with the earlier passage, allows himself an overlap of three syllables instead of one.

Ποσειδάν, ἐπεί νιν καθαροῦ λέβητος ἔξελε Κλωθώ

Ποσειδάν—ἄριστον: the reminiscence is unmistakable. And it is deliberate, because what follows is a repetition of the Aeolian couplet with which the strophe began. The only difference is that there the Glyconic and Pherecratic were independent, here they overlap. The return to the opening subject has been anticipated, but it is not yet complete.

ἐλέφαντι φαίδιμον ὦμον κεκαδμένον.

ἦ θαύματα πολλά, καί πού τι καὶ βροτῶν

φάτις ὑπὲρ τὸν ἀλαθῆ λόγον

The poet is playing with that Pherecratic-iambic motive with which we are now thoroughly acquainted, and thus holds us in suspense before his conclusion. The first two Pherecratics are varied by anacrusis—echoing rising rhythm, while the third is resolved in such a way as to echo Paeonic. And now for the conclusion:

δεδαιδαλμένοι ψεύδεσι ποικίλοις ἐξαπατῶντι μῦθοι.

Ποσειδάν, ἐπεί νιν. . . As before, we hear an initial bacchius, but this time the Aeolian couplet which follows is uncondensed, like the opening of the strophe: ἄριστον μὲν ὕδωρ, ὁ δὲ χρυσὸς αἰθόμενον πῦρ[1].

The first subject, then, is the Aeolian couplet, with which the composition begins and ends. In the middle we are intro-

---

[1] An exact parallel, in *poetical* composition, to this anticipation of the full return to the opening subject has been pointed out to me by Mr Sheppard in the opening paragraph of the *Oresteia*: 1 ἀπαλλαγὴν πόνων...19 διαπονουμένου, 20 ἀπαλλαγὴ πόνων.

duced to the second subject—Paeonic; and the transition from the one to the other is in both cases effected by trochaic and iambic. In other words the design is an elaboration of Three-part form on the lines of the modern *Rondo*: A–C–B–C–A. Thus, the metrical composition of this poem is not haphazard, as we might be led to suppose from the silence of most metricians, who content themselves with distinguishing and labelling the various phrases without attempting to consider the design as a whole: it is artistic, being based on definite principles of musical form. Can we say any more than this? Pindar is telling a story with a musical accompaniment, and we have seen that this accompaniment is artistically designed. Can we say that it is in any special sense appropriate to its subject?

The principal rhythms employed are Aeolian, Paeonic, trochaic and iambic, with a touch of Dorian and a still slighter touch of Ionian. As was explained in the last chapter, most of these rhythms were conventionally associated with different feelings or ideas. Is there any trace of those associations here? If so, we shall hardly expect them to recur with each recurrence of the corresponding rhythm—triadic form is too strict a convention to allow of so close a conformity as that between sense and rhythm: but do they recur often enough to suggest that the poet is deliberately using significant rhythm to heighten his effects? We shall remember, moreover, that such associations probably depended on melody as much as on rhythm; and this would enable the poet to enforce the significance of his rhythms, where he wants to enforce it, to disguise it where it is of no use to him.

Let us begin with the Aeolian rhythms. The Aeolian couplet is the rhythm of one of the best-known Greek wedding-songs:

'Υμήν, ὦ ὑμέναι' 'Υμήν, 'Υμὴν ὦ ὑμέναι' ὤ.

I hope to show later how Aeschylus uses the couplet with the significance it had acquired from popular association with the idea of marriage or love; and, presumably, when he used the popular rhythm, he used the popular melody too[1]. So here: in three passages, each of which describes an important step in the progress of the story, the Aeolian couplet is associated with love or marriage.

Poseidon falls in love with Pelops:

(40–1)　τότ' ἀγλαοτρίαιναν ἁρπάσαι,
　　　　δαμέντα φρένας ἱμέρῳ, χρυσέαισί τ' ἀν' ἵπποις . . .

Here the suggestion in the music of the Love-motive is only slight: but it is clearer in the second passage. Pelops falls in love with Hippodameia:

(69–71)　ἑτοῖμον ἀνεφρόντισεν γάμον
　　　　Πισάτα παρὰ πατρὸς εὔδοξον Ἱπποδάμειαν
　　　　σχεθέμεν.

And the third time, when, after the contest with Oenomaus, he wins his bride, the wedding-tune rings out in full force,—

(88)　ἕλεν δ' Οἰνομάου βίαν παρθένον τε σύνευνον.

The other Aeolian rhythm employed in this poem is the trochaic-Pherecratic couplet familiar to us from the Partheneion of Alcman:

Alcm. 23. 36–40

ἔστι τις σιῶν τίσις. ὁ δ' ὄλβιος ὅστις εὔφρων
ἀμέραν διαπλέκει ἄκλαυστος. ἐγὼν δ' ἀείδω . . .

It is a light, tripping measure, with the connotation common to most Aeolian rhythms—merrymaking, festivity and song.

(3–4)　εἰ δ' ἄεθλα γαρύεν / ἔλδεαι, φίλον ἦτορ, ...

(14–17)　ἀγλαΐζεται δὲ καὶ μουσικᾶς ἐν ἀώτῳ,
　　　　οἶα παίζομεν φίλαν ἄνδρες ἀμφὶ θαμὰ τράπεζαν.

---

[1] Euripides puts a reminiscence of the same popular refrain on the lips of his mad Cassandra—in conjunction with Paeonic, in allusion to the Aeschylean Cassandra (Eur. *Tro.* 307–24). Cf. also Eur. *Hcld.* 917–18, *I. A.* 1056–7, 1078–9, *Hipp.* 554.

(43-5) ἔνθα δευτέρῳ χρόνῳ / ἦλθε καὶ Γανυμήδης
        Ζηνὶ τωὖτ᾽ ἐπὶ χρέος.

(61-3) ἀλίκεσσι συμπόταις νέκταρ ἀμβροσίαν τε
        δῶκεν, ...

(90-2) νῦν δ᾽ ἐν αἱμακουρίαις ἀγλααῖσι μέμικται
        Ἀλφεοῦ πόρῳ κλιθείς, ...

Thirdly, let us follow through the poem that Dorian figure
we noted at the beginning of the strophe. Dorian rhythm, we
remember, is appropriate to manliness and courage among
men, and to Zeus among gods.

(2)   ἅτε διαπρέπει νυκτὶ μεγάνορος ἔξοχα πλούτου.

(13) Σικελίᾳ, δρέπων μὲν κορυφὰς ἀρετᾶν ἀπὸ πασᾶν,...

(42) ὕπατον εὐρυτίμου ποτὶ δῶμα Διὸς μεταβᾶσαι.

(89) τέκε τε λαγέτας ἐξ ἀρεταῖσι μεμαότας υἱούς.

Each strophe culminates in Paeonic—a strenuous, excited
rhythm well adapted to convey the idea of speed:

(20-2) ὅτε παρ᾽ Ἀλφεῷ σύτο δέμας
        ἀκέντητον ἐν δρόμοισι παρέχων,
        κράτει δὲ προσέμειξε δεσπόταν.

(77-8) ἐμὲ δ᾽ ἐπὶ ταχυτάτων πόρευσον ἁρμάτων
        ἐς Ἆλιν, κράτει δὲ πέλασον.

(93-6) τὸ δὲ κλέος
        τηλόθεν δέδορκε τᾶν Ὀλυμπιάδων ἐν δρόμοις
        Πέλοπος, ἵνα ταχυτὰς ποδῶν ἐρίζεται
        ἀκμαί τ᾽ ἰσχύος θρασύπονοι.

Among the dramatists, as we shall see, this rhythm is
constantly used with a sinister suggestion of impending
tragedy. So here, in the second antistrophe, where (not without playfulness) the poet alludes in hushed tones to the
slanderous story of the cannibal banquet of the gods, the
horror of the scene is heightened by the Paeonic accompaniment:

(47–51) ἔννεπε κρυφᾷ τις αὐτίκα φθονερῶν γειτόνων
ὕδατος ὅτι τε πυρὶ ζέοισαν εἰς ἀκμὰν
μαχαίρᾳ τάμον κατὰ μέλη,
τραπέζαισί τ᾽, ἀμφὶ δεύτατα, κρεῶν
σέθεν διεδάσαντο καὶ φάγον.

To feel the full significance of these rhythms you must take them with their context. Read the poem through, therefore, noting how the amorous couplet gives place to the manly or solemn Dorian, and that, in turn, to festive Aeolian, and to rapid Paeonic. These delicate transitions of rhythm and of feeling are to my mind among the most beautiful features of the poem.

(41–4) δαμέντα φρένας ἱμέρῳ, χρυσέαισί τ᾽ ἀν᾽ ἵπποις
Love

ὕπατον εὐρυτίμου ποτὶ δῶμα Διὸς μεταβᾶσαι·
Olympus

ἔνθα δευτέρῳ χρόνῳ ἦλθε καὶ Γανυμήδης
Festivity

(88–91) ἕλεν δ᾽ Οἰνομάου βίαν παρθένον τε σύνευνον·
Love

τέκε τε λαγέτας ἐξ ἀρεταῖσι μεμαότας υἱούς.
Valour

νῦν δ᾽ ἐν αἱμακουρίαις ἀγλααῖσι μέμικται....
Festivity

To have woven all the types of rhythm known to Greek lyric into a single musical design is in itself a feat of no mean artistic skill: but Pindar has done more than this—he has handled them with such delicacy that each serves to throw into relief the varying emotional effects of the poetry. We shall not grudge him, therefore, the praise which he bestows upon himself at the end of this remarkable composition:

πρόφαντον σοφίᾳ καθ᾽ Ἕλλανας ἐόντα παντᾷ.

CHAPTER EIGHT

THE SUPPLIANTS *OF AESCHYLUS*

ESCHYLUS learnt not a little of his tragic art from the
lyric poets : that is to say, he took over the technique
of choral lyric and adapted it to the needs of drama. In the
Oresteia this process of adaptation is complete : the long
choral odes are worked with such skill into the dramatic
framework that they are no less essential to the effect of the
whole than the action of the plot itself. In *The Suppliants*—
the earliest of his extant plays—the lyrical element is as yet
imperfectly assimilated. Regarded as lyrical compositions,
the choral odes of that play are perfect, but they are static
in quality rather than dynamic—more like the odes of Pindar
or Bacchylides than those of the *Agamemnon.*

A minor example of the advance made by Aeschylus as an
artist between the earliest and the latest of his extant compositions will be found in his treatment of significant rhythm.
We noticed in our study of the first Olympian that the triadic
convention in which that poem is written is such that the poet
cannot avail himself of the associative value of each rhythm
every time it recurs. The tragedians abandoned this convention of the repeated triad. They occasionally use a single
triad—a strophe, antistrophe, and epode—but it is never repeated; and in general they prefer the dyadic system of
strophe and antistrophe, without an epode, each successive
strophe being different from the last. No doubt, they chose
this form because it was the most flexible. Even so, however,
it required no little skill to make the rhythms of both strophe
and antistrophe equally effective, when, as often happened, the
sense of the words was entirely different. In several passages in
The Suppliants, for example, we find a coincidence of rhythm
and idea which holds good for the strophe but not for the

antistrophe, or good for the antistrophe but not for the strophe. This difficulty will appear less serious in the light of what has been said about melody, which could be used to enforce a significant rhythm, to disguise an irrelevant one. Still, it is awkward. But I believe that this awkwardness was felt by Aeschylus himself. He wrote this play at a time when he had not yet mastered the art of antistrophic composition as a dramatic medium. In the *Oresteia*—nearly forty years later—he has completely mastered that art, and contrives with amazing skill to make the two identical patterns of strophe and antistrophe serve with equal efficacy two entirely different purposes.

The fifty Danaids[1]—descendants of Io, the bride of Zeus— have sought refuge in Argos, the birthplace of their great ancestress, from their fifty cousins, the sons of Aegyptus, who seek to marry them against their will. They appeal for protection to Zeus, who brought the wanderings of their ancestress to a happy consummation, and to Pelasgus, the King of Argos: and in both cases they threaten, if their prayers are not answered, to kill themselves at the altars of the Argive gods. Pelasgus grants them protection, and the Herald sent by the sons of Aegyptus to demand their sur- render is forced to retire in discomfiture. The Suppliants are escorted amid rejoicing to their new homes, and all ends happily—for the time. The remainder of the trilogy is lost, but we know that their confidence in the protection of Zeus is misplaced: in the sequel he rejected their prayer, because it conflicted with other and greater designs of his own.

The dominant theme of the play is Zeus—the lover of Io and the greatest of the gods, the inscrutable governor of the destinies of man. It is from Zeus that the whole trilogy de- rives its significance, and around his name that the composition is designed. The shape the play is to take is clearly outlined in the anapaestic *parodos* (1–39), which is arranged as follows:

---

[1] In this account of the form and dramatic significance of *The Suppliants* I am following Mr Sheppard. See Preface, p. vii.

A Zeus the Suppliant.
B   Egypt.
A Epaphus, child of Zeus and Io.
C   Argos.
A Zeus and the Gods of the Dead.
    Invocation.

The form of the first stasimon (40–181) is similar: the opening theme is taken from the *middle* of the preceding anapaests, and in the middle of the stasimon we are introduced to a new theme, Zeus the All-Highest:

A Epaphus, child of Zeus and Io.
B   Lamentation.
A Zeus the All-Highest.
C   Invocation.
A Zeus of the Dead.

The second stasimon (533–607) proceeds along similar lines. We begin and end with the middle theme of the preceding stasimon, and in the middle return to the theme of Epaphus:

A Zeus the All-Highest.
B   Invocation.
A Zeus and Io: birth of Epaphus.
B   Invocation.
A Zeus the All-Highest.

The third (638–717) is arranged somewhat differently, but the leading theme is still the name of Zeus, with which the Suppliants now couple that of Ares, in unconscious antici-pation of the bloodshed that is to come:

Zeus.
  Ares.
Zeus.
  Ares, Aphrodite.
Zeus.
  Artemis, Ares.
Zeus.
  Ares, Justice.

Let us turn back to the first stasimon. We have already
analysed the poetical form : let us now look at the rhythmical
form, and see how the two coincide. The Suppliants begin in
Dorian, for Zeus (40–57): then, as they turn to lamentation,
comparing their fate to that of the hapless nightingale, we
hear Ionic a minore and Aeolian (58–87). They remind themselves that the will of Zeus is inscrutable and incontestable :
the rhythm is again Dorian (88–101). They appeal to him to
exercise his will on their behalf—to smite their pursuers with
a storm which will swallow them up before they can reach
the shores of Argos. This is the climax of the Ode: the
Suppliants have worked themselves into a frenzy of religious
incantation, and the rhythm is accordingly dochmiac (110–59).
Their frenzy dies away: but they still have one shaft in their
quiver—if Zeus is deaf to their appeal, they will hang themselves at his altar ! The rhythm is not, as we might expect,
Dorian again, but a slow trochaic measure, the significance of
which will appear in due course (160–81).

Having grasped the significance of the stasimon as a whole
let us now examine it in detail, strophe by strophe, observing
how these rhythms grow out of one another, and taking note
of one or two others which have not been included in our
summary of the whole.

Str. 1¹. Two-part form : A–B. Dorian.

A νῦν δ' ἐπικεκλομένα Δῖον πόρτιν ὑπερπόντιον τιμάορ', ἶνιν
   Prosodiacs   Epitrites

B ἀνθονομούσας προγόνου βοὸς ἐξ ἐπιπνοίας
   Prosodiacs

   Ζηνός· ἔφαψιν ἐπωνυμίᾳ δ' ἐπεκραίνετο μόρσιμος αἰὼν

   εὐλόγως, Ἔπαφόν τ' ἐγέννασε.
   Epitrites

The first part (A) is Dorian of the simplest kind : two prosodiacs followed by two epitrites. The second part (B) repeats
this scheme in an enlarged form, with variations. Instead of

¹ 45. Ζηνός· ἔφαψιν Headlam: Ζηνὸς ἔφαψιν.

the two prosodiacs, we have two long dactylic phrases which arise out of the normal prosodiac by resolution of the final spondee: and instead of the two normal epitrites we have two variants of that foot: ⏓⏑ ⏓⏑⏑ and the protracted form ⏓⏑ ⏓–⏓[1]. Notice, too, that the second part began with that short form of the prosodiac which is identical with the choriambus (ἀνθονο-μού-). This gives us a starting-point for our second strophe.

Str. 2. Three-part: AB–C–AB.

εἰ δὲ κυρεῖ τις πέλας οἰωνοπολῶν ἔγγαιος οἶκτον ἀΐων
<u>(A) Choriambic</u>   (B) Trochaic

δοξάσει τις ἀκούειν
(C) Pherecratic

ὄπα τᾶς Τηρείας μήτιδος οἰκτρᾶς ἀλόχου κιρκηλάτου δ' ἀηδόνος.
<u>(A) Ionic a minore</u>   (B) Trochaic

Choriambic for prophecy[2]; Ionic a minore for the lament of the nightingale[3]. And Pherecratic as a shift between the two: like choriambic, it is in falling rhythm, but its last four syllables, marked off for this purpose by the division of words (τις ἀκούειν), suggest Ionic a minore. The trochaic cadences recall the epitrite cadences of the first strophe: they also prepare for a new development in the next strophe.

Str. 3[4]. Two-part: AB–AB.

τὼς καὶ ἐγὼ φιλόδυρτος Ἰαονίοισι νόμοισι
A

---

[1] For these variants, see Appendix. Note how this, and the two following strophes, obtain their coherence from similarity of cadence: ἔγγαιος οἶκτον ἀΐων = κιρκηλάτου δ' ἀηδόνος, etc. Cf. S. Macpherson, *Form in Music*, p. 64: "This illustrates a very important factor in the matter of obtaining coherence of musical design, viz. some sort of *repetition*, at a later period of a movement, of some figure or passage that has been heard earlier in its course. One of the simplest methods of carrying out this idea of repetition is for the cadence-bars of the first half of the piece to be reproduced—with change of key, where necessary—at the end of the second part." Cf. Aesch. *Supp.* 533–9 (p. 92), 547–55 (pp. 92–3), *Agam.* 738–48 (pp. 114–15), *Cho.* 22–31 (p. 121), and for further examples see Appendix.

[2] See above, pp. 58–9.   [3] p. 55.

[4] 73 εἰλοθερῇ Bothe: νειλοθερῇ. 76 δειμαίνουσ' ἀφόνου Headlam: δειμαίνουσα φίλους.

δάπτω τὰν ἀπαλὰν εἰλοθερῆ παρειὰν
_____
Pherecratic

ἀπειρόδακρύν τε καρδίαν· γοεδνὰ δ᾽ ἀνθεμίζομαι
_____   _____
Pherecratic¹   (B) Iambic

δειμαίνουσ᾽ ἀφόνου τᾶσδε φυγᾶς ἀερίας ἀπὸ γᾶς
_____ _____ _____
(A) Prosodiac   Choriambus Prosodiac

εἴ τις ἐστὶ κηδεμών.
_____
(B) Trochaic

The strophe opens with what sounds as if it were going to be an Ionic elegiac couplet²; but after the first half of the pentameter (δάπτω τὰν ἀπαλὰν) it turns into a Pherecratic. This figure is repeated, with anacrusis, leading to a phrase identical in form with the first cadence of the previous strophe: ἔγγαιος οἶκτον ἀΐων. There, coming after strongly marked falling rhythm, it sounded like trochaic: here, coming after the anacrusis of the Pherecratic, we are tempted to take it as iambic. The fact is, a change from falling to rising rhythm is impending, and this hint of iambic is a preparation for it. The next figure I have called a prosodiac: its function is to recall the announcement of the preceding sentence: δειμαίνουσ᾽ ἀφόνου = δάπτω τὰν ἀπαλάν. In the same way, the next figure but one, ἀερίας ἀπὸ γᾶς, reminds us of τὼς καὶ ἐγὼ φιλόδυρ-. The two figures are echoes, and in between them is set an echo of that choriambic movement which we have already heard twice since the ode began. Why does it recur here? It is a rapid measure, appropriate, as we have seen, to restless motion such as flight: and that is its connotation here, both in strophe and in antistrophe—

76–7   δειμαίνουσ᾽ ἀφόνου τᾶσδε φυγᾶς ἀερίας ἀπὸ γᾶς . . .

85–6   ἔστι δὲ κἀκ πολέμου τειρομένοις βωμὸς ἀρῆς φυγάσιν . .

¹ I take 74 καρδίαν as a disyllable: cf. 83 στυγόντες, and see Verrall, _Seven against Thebes_, p. 134.
² Headlam, _ad loc._

Str. 3¹. Two-part: A–B. Dorian.

<u>εἴθ' εἴη Διὸς εὖ παναληθῶς—Διὸς ἵμερος οὐκ εὐθήρατος ἐτύχθη·</u>
(A) Prosodiacs
<u>παντᾶ τοι φλεγέθει κἂν σκότῳ μελαίνᾳ ξὺν τύχᾳ μερόπεσσι</u>
(B) Prosodiac   Epitrites
λαοῖς.

The thoughts of the Suppliants return to Zeus: so does the rhythm. The second part of this strophe resembles the second part of the opening strophe, except that here the final epitrite is not protracted. We may also notice that the division of words in both passages (εὐλόγως, κἂν σκότῳ, ξὺν τύχᾳ) suggests a new rhythm—Paeonic.

Str. 5².

<u>ἰάπτει δ' ἐλπίδων ἀφ' ὑψιπύργων πανώλεις βροτούς,</u>
Bacchius + Cretic   Dochmiac   Dochmiac
<u>βίαν δ' οὔτιν' ἐξοπλίζει·</u>
Bacchius   Dochmiac
<u>τὰν ἄπονον δ' ἁρμονίαν ἥμενος ἀμ φρόνημά πως</u>
Choriambic   Glyconic
<u>αὐτόθεν ἐξέπραξεν ἔμπας ἑδράνων ἀφ' ἁγνῶν.</u>
Aeolian couplet

The Suppliants now begin their invocation in real earnest, and for the first time we hear Paeonic—at present the slow unresolved forms, ∪⏤⏤ and ∪⏤∪⏤⏤ rather than ⏑∪∪⏤ and ∪∪∪⏤∪⏤. In the middle of the strophe we hear another choriambic passage. This is for the sake of the antistrophe, where the Suppliants pray that their enemies may be afflicted with heaven-sent madness, driving them to ruin like the gadfly which persecuted Io (114–5)³:

δυσπαραβούλοισι φρεσίν, καὶ διανοιομαίνολιν
κέντρον ἔχων ἄφυκτον, ἄτας ἀπάταν μεταλγούς.

¹ 88 εἴθ' εἴη Headlam: εἰθείη.
² 106–7 So Headlam: τὰν ἄποινον δαιμονίων· ἥμενον ἄνω.
³ 114 διανοιομαίνολιν sugg. Headlam: διάνοιαν μαίνολιν. 115 So Tucker: ἄταν δ ἀπάτᾳ μεταγνούς.

88 GREEK LYRIC METRE

Str. 6¹. Two-part: A–B.

τοιαῦτα πάθεα μέλεα θρεομένα δ' ἐγὼ λιγέα βαρέα δακρυοπετῆ,
(A) Iambic

ἰή, ἰή, ἰηλέμοισιν ἐμφερῆ ζῶσα γόοις με τιμῶ.
(B) Pherecratic

This is the climax of the invocation: the Suppliants perform
a passionate dirge, rending their veils and beating their breasts.
The rhythm is iambic, largely resolved, which has been prepared for by the iambic figures of the preceding strophes.
That resolved iambic is the appropriate accompaniment for
such performances is shown by a number of parallel passages.
We shall come across more than one in the *Oresteia*: others
will be found in the *Persae* (1039–66), in *The Seven against
Thebes* (941–95), and in the *Alcestis* (86–7).

The sixth strophe is followed by a refrain². The first subject is Aeolian. There are two others: spondaic, and quick,
resolved Paeonic. A–BC–A.

ἰλέομαι μὲν 'Απίαν βοῦνιν· καρβᾶν' αὐδὰν εὖ, γᾶ, κοννεῖς.
(A) Glyconic   (B) Spondaic

πολλάκι δ' ἐμπίτνω λακίδι σὺν λινοσινεῖ Σιδονίᾳ καλύπτρᾳ.
(C) Dochmiac   Paeons   (A) Pherecratic

Str. 7. Two-part: AB–AB.

πλάτα μὲν οὖν λινορραφής τε δόμος ἅλα στέγων δορὸς
(A) Iambic   (B) Trochaic³

ἀχείματόν μ' ἔπεμπε σὺν πνοαῖς·
(A) Iambic

οὐδὲ μέμφομαι· τελευτὰς δ' ἐν χρόνῳ πατὴρ ὁ παντόπτας
(B) Trochaic

πρευμενεῖς κτίσειεν.

The religious fervour of the Suppliants begins to die away.
The iambics are no longer resolved, and give place to trochaic.

¹ 121 ἐμφερῆ Tucker: ἐμπρεπῆ.
² 123 βοῦνιν· καρβᾶν': βοῦνιν, καρβᾶνα δ'.
³ With resolution of the first foot to ease the shift from iambic.

The weak ending of the first figure (λινορραφής τε) anticipates the weak ending of the first trochaic figure (τελευτὰς δ'), and this in turn prepares us for the protraction of the next phrase (παντόπτας). The effect of these trochaic figures, coming as they do after the excited iambics, is slow and heavy. They also suggest, unless my ear deceives me, an undercurrent of that slow dochmiac rhythm which we heard in the two preceding strophes and will hear many times again before the play is over:

οὐδὲ μέμφομαι· τελευτὰς δ' ἐν χρόνῳ πατὴρ ὁ παντόπτας.

Str. 8. Trochaic

εἰ δὲ μή, μελανθὲς ἡλιόκτυπον γένος,

τὸν γάϊον, τὸν πολυξενώτατον Ζῆνα τῶν κεκμηκότων

ἰξόμεσθα σὺν κλάδοις, ἀρτάναις θανοῦσαι,

μὴ τυχοῦσαι θεῶν Ὀλυμπίων.

This trochaic measure is a favourite with Aeschylus. He employs it many times in the *Oresteia* and again in the *Persae* (117–28)—mostly with the connotation of sinister foreboding or suspense. In the *Persae*, it is contrasted with the sweeping Ionics a minore which preceded it; here it offers no less striking a contrast to the resolved iambics and Paeonic which marked the height of the invocation. This last strophe is, as it were, an afterthought. The Suppliants threaten to kill themselves if their appeal is not granted. At the beginning of the stasimon they appealed to the son of Zeus, Epaphus— in Dorian rhythm; in the middle, to Zeus—again in Dorian; now they threaten to appeal to another Zeus—the King of the Dead, and accordingly the Dorian rhythm, which we might have expected to recur in this passage, is abandoned in favour of these slowly-moving, ominous trochaics.

Danaus, who has listened to his daughters' prayer in silence, now espies an approaching chariot and warns them to take sanctuary at the altar of the gods. The chariot appears,

bringing Pelasgus, King of Argos, who questions the new-
comers as to their origin and business. They appeal to him,
as they appealed to Zeus, for protection. Pelasgus hesitates.
They renew their appeal in a short lyrical dialogue (350–411),
containing three strophes from the Chorus, which are answered
by Pelasgus in iambic trimeters. The main theme is quick,
resolved dochmiac—a development of the dochmiac movement which we heard in the latter part of the first stasimon.
The first strophe contains an admixture of Aeolian; the
second is in dochmiac almost throughout, and a touch of
Aeolian duly returns in the third.

Str. 1. Two-part: AB–AB.

Παλαίχθονος τέκος, κλῦθί μου πρόφρονι καρδίᾳ, Πελασγῶν ἄναξ.
(A) Iambic   Cretic   Dochmiacs

ἴδε με τὰν ἱκέτιν φυγάδα περίδρομον λυκοδίωκτον ὡς
(B) Aeol. tripody[1]   (A) Dochmiac

     δάμαλιν ἂμ πέτραις

ἠλιβάτοις, ἵν' ἀλκᾷ πίσυνος μέμυκε φράζουσα βοτῆρι μόχθους.
(B) Aeol. tripody   Aeolian couplet

Str. 2. The second strophe is pure dochmiac, except for a
single phrase: A–B–A.

σύ τοι πόλις, σὺ δὲ τὸ δήμιον, πρύτανις ἄκριτος ὤν,
A

κρατύνεις βωμόν, ἑστίαν χθονός, μονοψήφοισι νεύμασιν σέθεν,

μονοσκήπτροισι δ' ἐν θρόνοις χρέος πᾶν ἐπικραίνεις·
                    (B) Prosodiac

ἄγος φυλάσσου.
A

The exception is that prosodiac: πᾶν ἐπικραίνεις. Zeus, the
Suppliants declared in their previous appeal, is omnipotent:
he governs the world from his heavenly throne. He has the
power to succour: let him exercise it, and so avert bloodshed
on his altars! Now they appeal to Pelasgus. He too, in his

---

[1] 352 ἴδε με shift by resolution.

own kingdom, is omnipotent; his nod, like the nod of Zeus, knows no gainsaying; seated upon his royal throne, he controls the destinies of Argos. Let him too avert bloodshed on his altars! Clearly, the Suppliants are drawing a parallel between the King of Heaven and the King of Argos : they assume that they have won the heavenly King to their side, and use this assumption to win the goodwill of the earthly king. This slight reminiscence of the Dorian rhythm which accompanied their appeal to Zeus adds force to the parallel.

The third and last strophe brings the lyrical dialogue to a close with a reminiscence of the Aeolian rhythm we heard in the first[1]. Three-part: A–B–A.

μήτι ποτ᾽ οὖν γενοίμαν ὑποχείριος κράτεσιν ἀρσένων.
(A) Aeolian tripodies[2]   (B) Dochmiac

ὕπαστρον δέ τοι μῆχαρ ὁρίζομαι γάμου δύσφρονος

φυγάν. ξύμμαχον δ᾽ ἑλομένος Δίκαν, κρῖνε σέβας τὸ πρὸς θεῶν.
                                (A) Pherecratic

The King still hesitates, whereupon the Suppliants address to him a short stasimon (423–46), mainly in cretics[3], with a few paeons and dochmiacs. Finally, in the dialogue which ensues, they reiterate their threat of suicide, and Pelasgus departs to consult his people.

The Suppliants turn once more to Zeus. Their first appeal culminated in slow dochmiac, leading to quick dochmiac at the height of the invocation. They have appealed to Pelasgus in the same rhythm—quick dochmiac. The second stasimon (533–607) carries on the development of this dochmiac motive. The Dorian and Aeolian of the earlier strophes are freely mixed with slow dochmiac; and the climax comes in the last

---

[1] 400 φυγάν Heath: φυγαί.

[2] These Aeolian tripodies might of course be taken as dochmiacs with a long initial syllable (see p. 12) like 399 μῆχαρ ὁρίζομαι. But the initial syllables are long in the antistrophe as well, whereas 399 μῆχαρ ὁρίζομαι corresponds to 409 ἄδικα μὲν κακοῖς: therefore I prefer to take them as Aeolian.

[3] See above, p. 67 n. 1.

strophe, which is slow dochmiac throughout. Thus, at the end of the stasimon, we still await a further climax—quick dochmiac.

The second stasimon begins, like the first, with the name of Zeus; and the opening strophe is so contrived as to combine the leading themes—Aeolian and dochmiac—with Dorian. It is held together by the twice-repeated Pherecratic cadence, and its form might be stated thus: ABC–AC–BC.

Str. 1^1 (533–9)

Iambo-choriambic   (B) Prosodiac
ἄναξ ἀνάκτων, μακάρων μακάρτατε καὶ τελέων
(A) Dochmiac

Prosodiac
τελειότατον κράτος, ὄλβιε Ζεῦ,
     (C) Pherecratic

               (C) Pherecratic
πιθοῦ τε καὶ γένει σῷ ἄλευσον ἀνδρῶν ὕβριν εὖ στυγήσας·
(A) Dochmiac

λίμνᾳ δ᾽ ἔμβαλε πορφυροειδεῖ τὰν μελανόζυγ᾽ ἄταν.
(B) Prosodiac   (C) Pherecratic

The opening phrase, it will be observed, is an iambo-choriambic: ἄναξ ἀνάκτων, μακάρων. Its function here is to suggest simultaneously dochmiac (ἄναξ ἀνάκτων) and prosodiac (-των, μακάρων). It is used, somewhat similarly, as an introduction to Dorian in the *Trachiniae* (94), where it anticipates the iambo-choriambic movement of the second strophe (116–8).

Str. 2 (547–55)

παλαιὸν δ᾽ εἰς ἴχνος μετέσταν ματέρος ἀνθονόμους ἐπωπάς,
Dochmiac   Aeolian decasyllable

λειμῶνα βούχιλον, ἔνθεν Ἰὼ οἴστρῳ ἐρεσσομένα
Dochmiac   Prosodiac

φεύγει ἁμαρτίνοος, πολλὰ βροτῶν διαμειβομένα

---

^{1} 536 καὶ γένει σῷ Schütz: καὶ γενέσθω.

φῦλα, διχῇ δ' ἀντίπορον γαῖαν ἐν αἴσᾳ διατέμνουσα πόρον
Choriambic
Pherecratic

κυματίαν ὁρίζει.
(*contd.*)

This strophe, like the last, is loosely constructed; it owes
what coherence it has to the two Pherecratic cadences: for
the latter part of the Aeolian decasyllable at the end of the
first sentence, ἀνθονόμους ἐπωπάς, is equivalent to a Pherecratic, and this is recalled by the Pherecratic at the end. The
first part of the same figure, ματέρος ἀνθονόμους, leads to the
prosodiacs which occupy the centre of the strophe, and out of
these (ἀνθονόμους, πολλὰ βροτῶν) is developed choriambic.
The last time we heard choriambic was in the first stasimon,
where it was used for the frenzy of the prophet, and later for
the flight of fugitives from battle, and for the divine persecution
of the wicked sons of Aegyptus. Here, both in strophe and
antistrophe, it is used for the wanderings of the frenzied Io,
and its occurrence is sufficiently striking to be regarded as
something in the nature of a climax. It is, in fact, the consummation of the scattered choriambic themes of the first
stasimon.

Str. 3¹ (565–73). Two-part: AB–AB.

ἱκνεῖται δὴ σινουμένα βέλει βουκόλου πτεροέντος
(A) Dochm. Iambic   (B) Pherecratic
Δῖον πάμβοτον ἄλσος,
Pherecratic

λειμῶνα χιονόβοσκον, ὄντ' ἐπέρχεται
Iambic trimeter

Τυφῶ μένος, ὕδωρ τὸ Νείλου νόσοις ἄθικτον,
Link²   Dochmiac

μαινομένα πόνοις ἀτίμοις ὀδύναις τε κεντροδαλήτισι θυιὰς ῞Ηρας.
Glyconic   Aeolian couplet

---

¹ 565 δὴ σινουμένα Headlam: δ' εἰσικνουμένου.

² − − ◡ − a figure not uncommon in dochmiac: see Appendix.

That short but arresting phrase Τυφῶ μένος aptly describes the monster Typho. The strophe ends with an Aeolian couplet. The same couplet at the end of the antistrophe (580–2) asks a question:

καὶ τότε δὴ τίς ἦν ὁ θέλξας πολύπλαγκτον ἀθλίαν οἰστρο-
δόνητον Ἰώ;

The answer is given in the next strophe: Zeus. And as the Suppliants allude to the mysterious union of Zeus with Io, we hear once more the Aeolian couplet, which cannot fail to remind us of the happy tune: Ὑμὴν ὦ ὑμέναι' Ὑμήν, Ὑμὴν ὦ ὑμέναι' ὦ.

Str. 4¹ (583–9). AB–AB–AB. Dochmiac and iambic, and Aeolian.

δι' αἰῶνος κρέων ἀπαύστου ⟨⏌‒ ⏌∪∪ ⏌‒⟩
(A) Dochmiac ———————   (B) Pherecratic

βίᾳ δ' ἀπηματοσθένει καὶ θείαις ἐπιπνοίαις
(A) Iambic ———————   (B) Pherecratic

παύεται, δακρύων δ' ἀποστάζει πένθιμον αἰδῶ.
Aeolian couplet

λαβοῦσα δ' ἔρμα Δῖον ἀψευδεῖ λόγῳ γείνατο παῖδ' ἀμεμφῆ.
(A) Iambic trimeter ———————   (B) Pherecratic

In the last strophe the singers return to the solemn thought of the omnipotent will of Zeus. The rhythm marks the consummation of the dochmiac movement which has run through the whole stasimon.

Str. 5² (598–602). Dochmiac, and iambic. Three-part: A–B–A.

---

¹ δι' Hermann: Ζεὺs. 584 βίᾳ δ' ἀπηματοσθενεῖ Headlam: βία δ' ἀπημάντῳ σθένει.
² 600. ⟨αὐτὸς⟩ αὐτόχειρ Voss: cf. Schol ad *loc*. αὐτὸς ὁ πατὴρ φυτουργὸς τοῦ γένους, ὁ τῇ ἑαυτοῦ χειρὶ θεραπεύσας τὴν Ἰώ. So Soph. *Ant*. 52 αὐτὸς αὐτουργῷ χερί. Thus the verse is an iambic trimeter: cf. 568, 588. Most editors have assumed a lacuna before πατήρ: εὖτέ γε Hermann, ἔστι δὲ Schwerdt, αὐτὸς ὁ Heimsoeth, εἰ γὰρ or even σὺ γὰρ Tucker. All these conjectures, except Tucker's, are attempts to reconcile the metre of this verse with that of 605 οὗτινος (corr. in

τίν' ἂν θεῶν ἐνδικωτέροισιν κεκλοίμαν εὐλόγως ἐπ' ἔργοις;
(A) Dochmiac

πατὴρ φυτουργὸς αὐτὸς αὐτόχειρ ἄναξ,
(B) Iambic trimeter

γένους παλαιόφρων μέγας τέκτων, τὸ πᾶν μῆχαρ οὔριος Ζεύς.
Iambic   (A) Dochmiac

I have analysed the last two figures as a dochmiac and a
trochaic dipody. They might equally well be regarded as
dochmiac: μέγας τέκτων, τὸ πᾶν μῆχαρ οὔριος Ζεύς. The fact
is that both rhythms are heard: the second stasimon ends
with an echo of the slow trochaic movement which was heard
at the end of the first.

Danaus, who accompanied Pelasgus on his mission to the
people of Argos, now returns, and announces that the Suppliants
are safe—Argos has granted them protection. They reply with
a hymn of thanksgiving, in which they pray the gods to prosper
the city which has consented to defend them from their
enemies (638–717). The rhythmical structure of this ode is
too simple to need detailed analysis here. The principal
subject is Aeolian, with which we are already acquainted as
the accompaniment of festivity and rejoicing; but we hear
beneath this cheerful Aeolian a more sinister motive—quick
dochmiac. It appears in the first strophe (Three-part:
A Aeolian, B Dochmiac, A Aeolian); it is abandoned in the
second, which is entirely Aeolian; but re-appears in the
third (Two-part: A Aeolian, B Dochmiac); while the last
strophe is in slow dochmiac, like the last of the previous
stasimon. It is, as it were, a running comment on this pre-
mature rejoicing, and drives home a sinister effect in the

ὅστινος M) ἄνωθεν ἡμένου σέβει κάτω. But it is the latter verse that is unrhythmical: I can find no parallel for a first paeon followed by iambi in this fashion.
οὔτινος is probably a gloss on ὅτου (cf. schol. ad Eur. *Hec.* 353). For κάτω Bamberger suggested κράτη, Heath κράτος (cf. *Agam.* 270). In the previous verse
(604) the Schol. seems to have read κρατύνων for κρατύνει codd. (Paley, Oberdick).
I therefore propose: (602–5)...Ζεύς, ὑπ' ἀρχᾶς οὔτινος θοάζων (τὸ μεῖον κρεισσόνων
κρατύνων) ὅτου κάτωθεν ἥμενος σέβει κράτη.

words themselves—the constant harping on the name of the God of bloodshed. And, in the slow dochmiacs of the last strophe, the Suppliants bring their song to an end with the reflection that one of the cardinal duties of man is obedience to his parents. In the sequel they are destined, despite their prayers, to marry their cousins; and, at their father's command, they will murder them on the wedding-night.

Quick dochmiac, then, which was abandoned in the last stasimon, is creeping in again. But the climax of this stasimon, as of the last, is still slow dochmiac. We feel that the rhythmical design is moving towards a further climax in continuous quick dochmiac.

Hardly is their song of rejoicing at an end when Danaus sights the sons of Aegyptus sailing into the bay. Seized with terror, the Suppliants cluster round their father, who seeks in vain to calm their fears with the assurance that it will be some time yet before their cousins can bring their ship to harbour and disembark. Finally, despite his daughters' protests, he departs to summon help from the city. The scene is partly lyrical, the Suppliants expressing their terror in quick dochmiac, their father seeking to reassure them in iambic trimeters. It corresponds therefore to the earlier scene in which the Suppliants appealed to Pelasgus; and just as that scene marked the first climax of the quick dochmiac theme, so this marks the second. And, like the earlier scene, it is followed by a short stasimon (784–831), in which the Suppliants, deserted, as they now are, without even their father to protect them, give themselves up to terror-stricken lamentation.

The first strophe is composed of themes with which we are already familiar—dochmiac and iambic, with a Pherecratic close. The second is important.

Str. 2 (800–7). Iambic and trochaic.

πόθεν δέ μοι γένοιτ' ἂν αἰθέρος θρόνος,
Iambic trimeter
πρὸς ὃν χιὼν ὑδρηλὰ γίγνεται νέφη,
Iambic trimeter

ἢ λισσὰς αἰγίλιψ ἀπρόσδερκτος οἰόφρων κρεμὰς

<u>Shift by anacrusis</u>   <u>Trochaic</u>

γυπιὰς πέτρα, βαθὺ πτῶμα μαρτυροῦσά μοι,

πρὶν δαΐκτορος βίᾳ καρδίας γάμου κυρῆσαι;

At the end of the first stasimon the Suppliants threatened to take refuge with the God of the Underworld rather than submit to the marriage they abhor. Now they wish they might throw themselves from a mountain-height rather than endure such a fate. The rhythm in both passages is the same; and, as if to drive home the significance of this coincidence between sense and rhythm, the idea of the strophe is repeated in the antistrophe (810–13):

τὸ γὰρ θανεῖν ἐλευθεροῦται φιλαιακτῶν κακῶν.
ἐλθέτω μόρος πρὸ κοίτας γαμηλίου τυχών.

The text of the next scene (832–921) is corrupt beyond hope of restoration, but the broader rhythmical effects are fairly clear. As soon as the Egyptian herald appears, the Suppliants express their abhorrence in free verse or ἀπολελυμένα (832–48), and the Herald, whose language is as uncouth as a villainous African's should be, replies in equally irregular verse, with a plentiful use of spondees and resolved dochmiacs (849–55):

οὐκοῦν οὐκοῦν τιλμοὶ τιλμοὶ καὶ στιγμοί,
πολυαίμων φόνιος ἀποκοπὰ κρατός . . .

We are reminded of the spondees which accompanied the hardly less barbaric utterances of the Suppliants themselves (124–5):

καρβᾶν᾽ αὐδὰν εὖ, γᾶ, κοννεῖς.

The Suppliants begin to lament, in Aeolian (856–7):

εἴθ᾽ ἀνὰ πολύρυτον ἀλμήεντα πόρον . . .

But their lamentations are interrupted by renewed outbursts of ἀπολελυμένα from the Herald (860–5, 872–7). As he repeats his threats, their cries become more hysterical. They acclaimed his coming with such exclamations as ὂ ὂ ὂ, ἄ ἄ ἄ (832) and ἠὲ ἠέ (844). Now they cry αἰαῖ αἰαῖ (878) and οἰοῖ οἰοῖ (887). The rhythm too becomes more passionate: Aeolian gives place to Ionic a minore (879–83)[1].

καὶ γὰρ δυσπαλάμως ὄλοιο
_____
Aeolian decasyllable

δι᾽ ἀλίρρυτον ἄλσος, κατὰ Σαρπηδόνιον χῶμα πολύψαμμον
_____
Shift   Ionic a minore

  ἀλαθεὶς
  ―――――――
  (contd.)

Εὐρείαισιν αὔραις.
_____
Pherecratic

The Herald is now carrying his threats into effect, and speaks with the calm determination of the iambic trimeter (893–5, 904–5, 914–15). The Suppliants reply in quick dochmiac— the final culmination of that motive,—and for the third time we hear those barbarous spondees as they utter a last appeal to Earth, Epaphus and Zeus (896–903)[2]:

οἰοῖ, πάτερ, βρέτεος ἄρος αὐάτα. μάλα δ᾽ ἄγει

ἄραχνος ὡς βάδην. ὄναρ ὄναρ μέλαν. ὀτοτοτοτοῖ.

μᾶ Γᾶ, μᾶ Γᾶ, βοᾶν φοβερὸν ἀπότρεπε, ὦ βᾶ Γᾶς παῖ Ζεῦ.

About to be carried off, they utter a cry of despair in the hope that the people of Argos may hear them:

(916) ἰὼ πόλεως ἀγοὶ πρόμοι, δάμναμαι.

(919)[3] διωλόμεσθ᾽· ἄσεπτ᾽, ἄναξ, πάσχομεν.

Danaus arrives with King Pelasgus in the nick of time, and the Herald is forced to retire. The King announces that quarters have been assigned to the Suppliants in the city, Danaus warns the young women not to abuse their privileges, and the play ends with a jubilant *exeunt omnes*. At least, they begin jubilantly, with a song of rejoicing: but their song is set to Ionic a minore—the rhythm of lamentation (1029–62). And as they leave for their new homes, we overhear a dialogue

[1] 883 Εὐρείαισιν Paley: εὐρείαις εἰν.

[2] 896 αὐάτα· ἅτα ex schol. Abresch. μάλα δ᾽ Bothe: μάλδα.

[3] 919 ἄσεπτ᾽ Tucker: ἄελπτ᾽.

among the Suppliants which shows that there are some whose
fears for the future have not been entirely allayed by their
recent triumph (1063–72).

Then the last strophe of the play:

Str. 3[1]. Three-part: A–B–A.

Ζεὺς ἄναξ ἀποστεροίη γάμον δυσάνορα δάϊον, ὥσπερ Ἰὼ
(A) Trochaic   (B) Pherecratic

πημονᾶς ἐλύσατ᾽ αὖ χειρὶ παιωνίᾳ κατάσχετον,
(A) Trochaic

εὐμενεῖ βίᾳ κτίσας..

"Zeus, avert this marriage, or we will hang ourselves at the
altar!" they cried, in trochaics, at the end of the first stasimon. "Rather than submit to this marriage, let us throw
ourselves from the mountain-tops!" they cried, again in
trochaics, just before the arrival of the Herald. And now
for the third time, "May Zeus avert this marriage!" The
alternative is not repeated in the words, but it is clearly
implied in the rhythm.

The sequel is lost, but we know from other sources what
form that alternative ultimately took. The women who appealed in the first play of the trilogy for protection with the
piteous cry (757):

γυνὴ μονωθεῖσ᾽ οὐδέν· οὐκ ἔνεστ᾽ Ἄρης—

are destined, in the second, to show not a little of that manly
spirit they professed to lack:

γυνὴ γὰρ ἄνδρ᾽ ἕκαστον αἰῶνος στερεῖ,
δίθηκτον ἐν σφαγαῖσι βάψασα ξίφος[2].

---

[1] 1075 ὥσπερ Auratus: ὅσπερ. 1076 αὖ Headlam: εὖ. 1077 κατάσχετον Weil:
κατασχέθων.

[2] *P. V.* 888–9.

CHAPTER NINE

THE ORESTEIA

OUR study of *The Suppliants* has shown that in order to appreciate fully the choral element in the play we must regard each ode, not as an independent unity, but as part of a larger musical design which runs parallel with the plot and accelerates or retards its pace in accordance with the dramatic necessities of the moment. But the play itself is not complete: it is only the first of three acts. In the same way, we may suppose that the musical design of the first play is no more than the first movement in a still larger design which embraces the trilogy as a whole. Direct proof of this, in the case of *The Suppliants*, is impossible, because the sequel is lost. If we want to see how Aeschylus welded his single plays into a trilogy, we must turn to the *Oresteia*—the only complete trilogy that we possess. There we shall find the same principles of composition at work, and we shall find that by this means not only is one ode bound to another, but each play bound to the next, like a three-panelled design in tapestry in which certain threads run through the whole. Or a closer analogy would be Wagner's great tetralogy, conceived on the Aeschylean model. There, each play stands out, a unity—to some extent—in itself, but at the same time part of a still greater unity; and the musical themes which were heard for the first time in *Rheingold* are heard again in *Die Walküre* and in *Siegfried*, and culminate in *Götterdämmerung*. Similarly, the design of the *Agamemnon*, and again of the *Choephoroe*, has a certain unity of its own, but at the same time it forms part of a larger unity which is not fully grasped till we have reached the end of the *Eumenides*; and the musical themes which we hear first in the *Agamemnon* we hear again in the *Choephoroe*, until they too reach their final consummation in the *Eumenides*.

Nevertheless, there are important differences of technique

between *The Suppliants* and the *Oresteia*—the sort of differences we should expect between an early and a late work,
between a simple and an elaborate composition. In the first
place, let us compare the poetical form of the two pieces. We
observed that the earlier odes of *The Suppliants* were designed
according to principles familiar to us from previous stages of our
enquiry, and that these designs were built out of a few simple
themes—Zeus in different aspects. The form of the later odes
was less precise: that was natural, because, while thematic
composition of this kind is helpful in expounding the dramatic
situation, and in providing a setting from which the plot begins
to take shape and move, it would be a hindrance if maintained
in the same degree of elaboration after the plot has gathered
impetus and has begun to advance with increasing rapidity
towards the climax. The composition of the earlier odes of
the *Agamemnon* is based on the same principles, but treated
with far greater subtlety. The transitions from one theme to
another are less obvious, and the themes themselves are less
clearly-defined, more numerous and various. They are therefore much harder to explain on paper. The attempt which
follows does not pretend to be complete. Only the leading
themes are taken into consideration, and even they are stated
with a definiteness which scarcely does justice to the subtle
skill with which they are introduced. That, however, is un-
avoidable in reducing to analysis so elaborate and so delicate
a composition. At the same time, the reader will feel, as he
passes from one ode to the next, that the emotional value of
each, and the dramatic connexion between them, owe something to the manner in which these themes are arranged[1].

First stasimon (104–269)
    A. Omen.
    B. Zeus chastens the sinner.
    A. Fulfilment of the omen.

[1] I owe this summary of the form of the *Agamemnon* to Mr Sheppard's valuable
account in *Aeschylus and Sophocles*, pp. 16–39: see also *Camb. Univ. Reporter*,
vol. LIX, no. 15, pp. 430–1.

Second stasimon (367–480)
B. Zeus has chastened the sinner, Paris.
C. Helen.
B. Zeus will chasten the sinner, Agamemnon.

Third stasimon (686–773)
C. Helen.
D. The lion's whelp.
C. Helen.

The second subject of each movement is restated as the first subject of the next. Is not this very similar to the structure of the early odes of *The Suppliants*, analysed in the last chapter, and are we not reminded of the *cyclic* form of some compositions in modern music?

We have noticed how the poetical form of *The Suppliants* is gradually relaxed, as the play progresses, in order that the plot may move more freely. The metrical form developes in the same way. In the early odes most of the strophes were found to be in strict Two-part or Three-part form: in the later, they were often more loosely constructed, though rarely without some hint of formal design, sufficient to satisfy an ear which had already grasped the more obvious unity of the earlier strophes. In the *Oresteia* we find that Aeschylus has advanced further along this line of development. Strophic form is now so familiar to himself and to his audiences that he can dispense with the more obvious indications of it and so allow himself greater freedom in composition. From time to time he gives us a strophe as strict as any in *The Suppliants*; and on these occasions we can see that he is deliberately retarding the dramatic movement. An excellent example will be found in the first stasimon (104–269). The first and third parts of this poem are loosely constructed—the one in flowing dactylic, the other in continuous dochmiac: in both he is telling a story— the marshalling of the host at Aulis, and the sacrifice of Iphigeneia; and nothing must be allowed to impede the swift march of events. But in the middle he makes a digression—

a meditation on the theme of Zeus who chastens the sinner—solemn in character and slow in movement,—a striking contrast to its setting. And here he gives us a strophe composed out of slow trochaic in regular Three-part form.

We have already had occasion to notice the variety of Dorian rhythm developed by Stesichorus[1]. Prosodiacs are combined to produce a single, long dactylic phrase, which has something of the sweep and fluency of the epic hexameter:

Stesich. 18

ᾤκτειρε γὰρ αὐτὸν ὕδωρ αἰεὶ φορέοντα Διὸς κούρα βασιλεῦσιν.

Sometimes the final spondees are replaced by dactyls, with the result that the prosodiac basis disappears entirely:

Ibid. 7

Σκύπφειον δὲ λαβὼν δέπας ἔμμετρον ὡς τριλάγυνον
πῖνεν ἐπισχόμενος, τό ῥά οἱ παρέθηκε Φόλος κεράσας.

Epitrites are rarer than is usual in Dorian, and when they occur have the effect of retarding the rhythm:

Ibid. 26

οὕνεκα Τυνδάρεος ῥέζων ποτε πᾶσι θεοῖς μούνας λάθετ᾽ ἠπιοδώρω
Κύπριδος· κεῖνα δὲ Τυνδαρέου κόραις
χολωσαμένη διγάμους τε καὶ τριγάμους τίθησιν
καὶ λιπεσάνορας . . .

It was in this form of Dorian that Stesichorus wrote his *Sack of Troy* and his *Oresteia*. Aeschylus makes the Sack of Troy one of the leading themes of the earlier part of his own *Oresteia*, and no doubt, for the Greek audience, the theme as he treated it derived not a little of its significance from the reminiscences it evoked in their minds of the work of Stesichorus. This is only another example of the habitual method of the Greek poets—they loved to enforce the effect of their own poetry by conscious allusion to their predecessors. In the

[1] See above, pp. 38, 48.

present case, the modern reader is at a disadvantage, because the work of Stesichorus has perished; but even we can see that Aeschylus begins his long first stasimon in the rhythm which Stesichorus had made familiar before him:

κύριός εἰμι θροεῖν ὅδιον κράτος αἴσιον ἀνδρῶν
ἐκτελέων· ἔτι γὰρ θεόθεν καταπνείει
πειθώ, μολπᾶν ἀλκάν, σύμφυτος αἰών·
ὅπως Ἀχαιῶν. . .

The first phrase is a dactylic hexameter; the next two move more slowly, because spondees are substituted for dactyls. The fourth is something new. Perhaps it is an epitrite with anacrusis[1]: but it suggests rising rhythm, and, as we shall see, its resemblance to slow dochmiac (◡⏌◡⏌–) is not without significance for the sequel (115–119).

οἰωνῶν βασιλεὺς βασιλεῦσι νεῶν, ὁ κελαινὸς ὅ τ' ἐξόπιν ἀργᾶς,
φανέντες ἴκταρ, μελάθρων χερὸς ἐκ δορυπάλτου. . .

At the end of the strophe (121–3) it leads to the climax:

βοσκόμενοι λαγίναν, ἐρικύματα φέρματι, γένναν,
βλαβέντα λοισθίων δρόμων.

This last phrase clearly suggests iambic, rising rhythm (◡⏌◡⏌ ◡⏌◡⏌), in striking contrast to the falling rhythm of the rapid dactylics which it interrupts. Read the strophe through again, and you will feel its emotional effect: by breaking the fluent movement of the dactylic narrative, it emphasises the sinister meaning conveyed in the words[2].

Now turn to the epode (146)[3]:

τόσον περ εὔφρων. . .

This is the same quasi-dochmiac phrase we heard in the strophe, and this time no dactylic phrases precede it to make us regard

---

[1] Cf. Terpand. 2 ἀμφί μοι αὖτε ἄναχθ' ἑκαταβόλον | ἀειδέτω φρήν.
[2] It has the same effect in the antistrophe (144) στυγεῖ δὲ δεῖπνον αἰετῶν.
[3] 146 τόσον f h, Headlam: τόσσον M.

it as an epitrite: its dochmiac character is becoming clearer. We continue in rising rhythm (146–7)[1]:

τόσον περ εὔφρων δὲ καλὰ δρόσοισι λεπτοῖς μαλερῶν λεόντων

The second figure is an Anacreontic. The effect is tender; and here again the sense of the words explains the rhythm. As he speaks of the "offspring of lions" the prophet is thinking of Iphigeneia, the daughter of the House of Mycenae, whose emblem was a lion[2]. Anacreontic will recur in this connexion.

The third figure μαλερῶν λεόντων brings this little excursion into rising rhythm to an end with a suggestion of a Pherecratic cadence (-οἷς μαλερῶν λεόντων)[3], and we return to the dactylic movement of the strophe (148–52)[4]:

πάντων τ' ἀγρονόμων φιλομάστοις
θηρῶν ὀβρικάλοις, εἴπερ τινά, τούτων αἴνει ξύμβολα κρᾶναι
δεξιὰ μέν, κατάμομφα δὲ φάσματ' ἀνορθοῦν.

That is the first sentence. The second begins (153), like the first, with a suggestion of Paeonic—even clearer this time:

ἰήϊον δὲ καλέω Παιᾶνα . . .

Two iambi; then a fourth paeon, as the prophet cries to Apollo the Healer; and then a palimbacchius (–⏑), which serves as a convenient shift back to falling rhythm (154–6):

μή τινας ἀντιπνόους Δαναοῖς χρονίας ἐχενηΐδας
ἀπλοίας τεύξῃ . . .

At first, dactyls, light and rapid; then that heavy spondaic prosodiac ⏑– ⏑– ⏑. The ships are storm-bound; the rhythm is held up. And then suddenly it quickens (157–63):

σπευδομένα θυσίαν ἑτέραν ἄνομόν τιν', ἄδαιτον,
νεικέων τέκτονα σύμφυτον, οὐ δεισήνορα· μίμνει

---

[1] 146 δὲ καλὰ δρόσοισι λεπτοῖς Headlam: ἁ καλὰ δρόσοισιν ἀέλπτοις.
[2] Headlam, *ad loc.*
[3] For this Ionian cadence, cf. below 214, 236 (p. 109), 451 (p. 111), *Cho.* 319 (p. 125).
[4] 149 ὀβρικάλοις εἴπερ τινὰ Headlam: ὀβρικάλοισι τερπνὰ. 150 αἴνει Gilbert: αἴτει. 152 φάσματ' ἀνορθοῦν Wecklein: φάσματα στρουθῶν.

γὰρ φοβερὰ παλίνορτος
οἰκονόμος δολία μνάμων μῆνις τεκνόποινος.

With that pregnant word (vengeance for a child? or of a child?) the rhythm, which has been gathering speed in the preceding phrases, comes to an abrupt stop. All that remains to do now is to round off the epode with a couple of smooth dactylic hexameters (164–7), which recall, both in sense and rhythm, the opening of the strophe:

τοιάδε Κάλχας ξὺν μεγαλοῖς ἀγαθοῖς ἀπέκλαγξεν
μόρσιμ᾽ ἀπ᾽ ὀρνίθων ὁδίων οἴκοις βασιλείοις.

And finally we hear the refrain, bringing the triad formally to a close (168–9):

τοῖς δ᾽ ὁμόφωνον
αἴλινον αἴλινον εἰπέ, τὸ δ᾽ εὖ νικάτω.

At this point the rhythm completely changes. Instead of long, sweeping dactylic, we hear that slow insistent trochaic measure which was used with such effect in *The Suppliants* (170–7)[1]:

Ζεύς, ὅστις ποτ᾽ ἐστίν, εἰ τόδ᾽ αὐτῷ φίλον κεκλημένῳ,
τοῦτό νιν προσεννέπω·
οὐκ ἔχω προσεικάσαι πάντ᾽ ἐπισταθμώμενος . . .

As the old men think of their only solace in the hour of trouble, their spirits rise and the rhythm quickens, returning for a moment to dactylic:

πλὴν Διός, εἰ τὸ μάταν ἀπὸ φροντίδος ἄχθος
χρὴ βαλεῖν ἐτητύμως.

The same effect is repeated in the antistrophe (183–5). The ancient rulers of the world—Ouranos, Kronos—have fallen, but Zeus—

Ζῆνα δέ τις προφρόνως ἐπινίκια κλάζων
τεύξεται φρενῶν τὸ πᾶν.

[1] For the form (three-part) see above, p. 40.

In the next strophe (186-93) the dactylic second subject is abandoned in favour of a still slower variety of trochaic:

A <u>τὸν φρονεῖν βροτοὺς ὁδώσαντα, τὸν πάθει μάθος</u>

    θέντα κυρίως ἔχειν.

B <u>στάζει δ' ἔν θ' ὕπνῳ πρὸ καρδίας μνησιπήμων πόνος</u>

    καὶ παρ' ἄκοντας ἦλθε σωφρονεῖν.

A <u>δαιμόνων δέ που χάρις βίαιος σέλμα σεμνὸν ἡμένων.</u>

The cretics in the middle of the second subject recall Paeonic rhythm (μνησιπήμων πόνος); and does not the end of the last figure but one (χάρις βίαιος) remind us of that slow dochmiac (τόσον περ εὔφρων) which we heard some time ago? The antistrophe (194-201) is even more remarkable. It describes how the storm came at Aulis: and the words are made to break across the phrases so as to produce in the rhythm a slow, heavy, straining effect exactly appropriate to the sense:

καὶ τόθ' ἡγεμὼν ὁ πρέσβυς νεῶν Ἀχαιικῶν,

    μάντιν οὔτινα ψέγων,

ἐμπαί-οις τύχαισι συμπνέων, εὖτ' <u>ἀπλοίᾳ κεναγγεῖ βαρύνοντ'</u>

    Ἀχαιικὸς λεὼς

Χαλκίδος πέραν ἔχων παλιρρόχ-θοις ἐν Αὐλίδος τόποις.

Note in particular how a suggestion of bacchii and iambic is made to run counter to the cretic and trochaic figures of the second subject: ἀπλοίᾳ | κεναγγεῖ | βαρύνοντ' | Ἀχαιικὸς λεώς. The effect is not merely to retard the rhythm; we have here a direct anticipation of the return to rising rhythm in the next strophe (202-3).

πνοαὶ δ' ἀπὸ Στρυμόνος μολοῦσαι

κακόσχολοι, νήστιδες, δύσορμοι . . .

ὅπως Ἀχαιῶν, φανέντες ἴκταρ, τόσον περ εὔφρων . . . The significance of those scattered hints of dochmiac is now clear: they have anticipated the dochmiac movement of the present strophe.

Here again the words break across the phrasing:

πνοαὶ δ' ἀπὸ Στρυμόνος μολοῦσαι

κακόσχολοι, νήστιδες, δύσορμοι . . .

Does not this straining effect, this tense struggle between dochmiac and trochaic, suggest as clearly as rhythm can the straining of the ropes as the fleet lies at anchor, pitching and rolling in the storm? Moreover, if the words Στρυμόνος μολοῦσαι, νήστιδες δύσορμοι recall the trochaic rhythm of the preceding strophe, the words πνοαὶ δ' ἀπὸ, κακόσχολοι anticipate the next figure:

βροτῶν ἄλαι, . . .

Then we return:

νεῶν τε καὶ πεισμάτων ἀφειδεῖς (◡⏑◡⏑– ◡⏑◡⏑–)

the same effect as before. And then, more slowly still:

παλιμμήκη χρόνον τιθεῖσαι (◡⏑–⏑ ◡⏑◡⏑–)

until at last a protracted dochmiac brings the rhythm to a halt:

τρίβῳ κατέξαινον ἄνθος Ἀργείων. (◡⏑◡⏑– ◡⏑◡⏑–⏑)[1]

The deadlock is complete, both in sense and rhythm. The situation seems hopeless: Artemis has frustrated the king's high enterprise. How can she be appeased?

ἐπεὶ δὲ καὶ πικροῦ . . .

Those iambics hold us in suspense for a moment: they are lighter, and we feel that we are moving towards a solution of the deadlock. Then the rhythm gathers speed: the prophet sees the way out, and his voice rises to a cry at the name of the offended goddess:

ἐπεὶ δὲ καὶ πικροῦ χείματος ἄλλο μῆχαρ βριθύτερον πρόμοισιν
Iambic   Pherecratic   Pherecratic

μάντις ἔκλαγξεν προφέρων Ἄρτεμιν . . .
Choriambic

[1] Cf. Soph. O.T. 1332 ἔπαισε δ' αὐτόχειρ νιν οὔτις ἀλλ' ἐγὼ τλάμων.

But the cure is worse than the disease; no sooner is it pre-
scribed than we hear the music of lamentation:

ὥστε χθόνα βάκτροις ἐπικρούσαντας Ἀτρείδας
‾‾‾‾‾‾‾‾‾‾‾‾‾‾‾‾‾‾‾‾‾‾‾‾‾‾‾‾‾‾‾‾‾‾‾‾‾
Shift[1] Ionic a minore

    δάκρυ μὴ κατασχεῖν.
    ‾‾‾‾‾‾‾‾‾‾‾‾‾‾
    Cadence[2]

Surely this is a remarkable composition. We hear in the
rhythm the storm-bound ships straining at their anchors, we
feel the spirit of despondency which oppresses the crews that
man them. Suddenly the ships are released, and our spirits
rise—but only to fall away into weeping and lamentation.

What of the antistrophe? It will, I think, show the art of
strophic composition at its height: Aeschylus has mastered
the difficulty which gave him trouble in *The Suppliants*.

(215–37)[3]
ἄναξ δ' ὁ πρέσβυς τόδ' εἶπε φωνῶν·
βαρεῖα μὲν κὴρ τὸ μὴ πιθέσθαι,
βαρεῖα δ' εἰ
τέκνον δαΐξω, δόμων ἄγαλμα,
μιαίνων παρθενοσφάγοισιν
ῥοαῖς πατρῴους χέρας πέλας βωμοῦ.

The straining effect being no longer required, the dochmiacs
are unbroken: instead, they are insistent in their monotony.
Agamemnon cannot make up his mind, and finally breaks
down, overcome at the thought of the terrible decision that
lies before him.

τί τῶνδ' ἄνευ κακῶν;

He is moving towards a decision: which will it be? Again, the

---

[1] If we looked only to the metrical pattern, we might take this phrase (212–3)
like the last as choriambic: but the words are so divided that they demand, to
my ear, to be taken as Ionic a minore.

[2] Cf. above 147 (p. 105) μαλερῶν λεόντων.

[3] 220 ῥοαῖς Schoemann: ῥείθροις h. 221 πέλας βωμοῦ Blomfield: βωμοῦ πέλας
(the more usual order: cf. Eur. *I. A.* 1426, *Andr.* 1157, *Hcld.* 73 βωμοῦ πέλας).

rhythm quickens; and he asserts that to betray his political allies is impossible, to shed his daughter's blood is—right!

πῶς λιπόναυς γένωμαι, ξυμμαχίας ἁμαρτών;
πανσανέμου γὰρ θυσίας παρθενίου θ' αἵματος ὀργᾷ
περιοργῶς ἐπιθυμεῖν θέμις· εὖ γὰρ εἴη.

The next strophe returns to dochmiac, now more sinister than ever—an ominous comment on the king's decision:

ἐπεὶ δ' ἀνάγκας ἔδυ λέπαδνον
φρενὸς πνέων δυσσεβῆ τροπαίαν
ἄναγνον, ἀνίερον . . .

Another climax: the resolved iambic suggests a fourth paeon (*ἀνίερον* ⏖⏑⏑⏑⏒). This is the second time we have heard that rhythm.

ἄναγνον, ἀνίερον, τόθεν
τὸ παντότολμον φρονεῖν μετέγνω.
βροτοὺς θρασύνει γὰρ αἰσχρόμητις
τάλαινα παρακοπὰ πρωτοπήμων.

ἀνίερον—παρακοπά: the dramatic significance of this fourth paeon is becoming clear. It is something to do with the heaven-sent madness which drives the man with blood on his hands to his own undoing.

ἔτλα δ' οὖν *θυτὴρ γενέσθαι* *θυγατρός, γυναικοποίνων*
Bacchius Dochmiac Anacreontic
πολέμων ἀρωγὰν *καὶ προτέλεια ναῶν.*
Shift Pherecratic

Again an Anacreontic—for Iphigeneia and Helen.

The last strophe, describing the sacrifice of Iphigeneia, is in dochmiac throughout except for the Pherecratic close—hence it marks a climax in the rhythm as well as in the narrative. The predominant phrase is still ⏑⏒⏑⏒– ⏑⏒⏑⏒– which has been heard with increasing frequency from the time of its introduction under the guise of epitrite among the dactylics of the opening strophe. But we also hear, for the first time, a second variety of the same rhythm: ⏑⏒–⏑⏒ (248 *ἀναύδῳ μένει*).

The second stasimon (379–480) begins by taking up the dochmiac climax of the first, thus leading us to suppose that this movement will be developed still further. In addition to ⏑–⏑–– ⏑–⏑–– we hear ⏑–́–́ ⏑–⏑––, ⏑–́–⏑–́ ⏑–⏑–– and other combinations of these elements. Towards the end of the first strophe (387–91) we pass through trochaic to Pherecratic, in preparation for the Aeolian refrain¹. The second strophe, also dochmiac, demands no comment, except perhaps for the concluding phrase (424):

φάσμα δόξει δόμων ἀνάσσειν.

This is dochmiac lopped, as it were, of its initial syllable (–́⏑–́– ⏑–́⏑–́– instead of ⏑–́⏑–́– ⏑–⏑––), so as to suggest trochaic (–́⏑–́ –́⏑–́⏑–́–), in anticipation of the trochaic movement of the third strophe (445–51):

ὁ χρυσαμοιβὸς δ᾽ Ἄρης σωμάτων
Dochmiac

καὶ ταλαντοῦχος ἐν μάχῃ δορὸς	πυρωθὲν ἐξ Ἰλίου
Trochaic	Dochmiac

φίλοισι πέμπει βαρὺ	ψῆγμα δυσδάκρυτον ἀν-
Dochmiac	Trochaic

τήνορος σποδοῦ γεμίζων λέβητας εὐθέτους.
(*contd.*)

At this point the rhythm shifts by anacrusis to iambic:

στένουσι δ᾽ εὖ λέγοντες ἄνδρα τὸν μὲν ὡς μάχης ἴδρις,

τὸν δ᾽ ἐν φοναῖς καλῶς πεσόντ᾽—

And then another shift which brings us, as we think of the woman who is the cause of all this bloodshed, to Anacreontic:

ἀλλοτρίας διαὶ γυναικός, τάδε σῖγά τις βαΰζει,
Anacreontic

φθονερὸν δ᾽ ὑπ᾽ ἄλγος ἕρπει προδίκοις Ἀτρείδαις.
Anacreontic   Cadence

The first stasimon worked slow dochmiac up to a climax, the second has maintained it as the predominant rhythm, the third and fourth will carry it still further.

¹ See above, p. 26.

The third stasimon (686–773) begins, gravely, in trochaic (686–701)[1]:

τίς ποτ᾽ ὠνόμαζεν ὧδ᾽ ἐς τὸ πᾶν ἐτητύμως·
μῆτις ὄντιν᾽ οὐχ ὁρῶμεν . . .

The third phrase has a weak ending. Having thrown out this hint of developments to come, the poet brings us back to the phrases with which the strophe began by making the last syllable of the third phrase do duty as the first of the next— an equally well-known trochaic rhythm:

μῆτις ὄντιν᾽ οὐχ ὁρῶμεν προνοίαισι τοῦ πεπρωμένου
γλῶσσαν ἐν τύχᾳ νέμων; τὰν δορίγαμβρον ἀμφινεικῆ θ᾽

That last phrase marks a further advance: the weak ending is repeated, and a dactyl is substituted for a trochee in the first foot. It prepares us for the sequel. Repeat it without its initial syllable, and we get an Anacreontic just in time to accompany the first mention of Helen's name in the play:

τὰν δορίγαμβρον ἀμφινεικῆ θ᾽ Ἑλέναν; ἐπεὶ πρεπόντως
_____
Anacreontic

Having thus passed from trochaic into Anacreontic, the rhythm undergoes another metamorphosis.

ἑλέναυς ἕλανδρος . . .

Another Anacreontic, you will say. But no: with the next word ἑλέπτολις we pass to Ionic a minore, the rhythm associated with the luxury (ἁβρότης) of Asia:

ἑλέναυς ἕλανδρος ἑλέπτολις ἐκ τῶν ἁβροτίμων
Shift   Ionic a minore

And then back to Anacreontic. Helen is wafted over the sea by the wind whose child was Love:

προκαλυμμάτων ἔπλευσεν Ζεφύρου γίγαντος αὔρᾳ,

_____

[1] This account of 686–717 is largely based on Headlam, *J. H. S.* vol. XXII, pp. 221–3.

The Greeks speed after her:

πολύανδροί τε φεράσπιδες κυναγοὶ κατ' ἴχνος πλατᾶν ἄφαντον
<u>Echo</u>

Then the rhythm slows down again as they beach their ships at Troy:

κελσάντων Σιμόεντος ἀκτὰς ἐπ' ἀεξιφύλλους
<u>Aeolian couplet[1]</u>

With this phrase—an effective final cadence—the strophe might have ended. Hence, if more is to follow, it is likely to be emphatic. We have yet to hear a horrified whisper:

δι' ἔριν αἱματόεσσαν.

It is another Pherecratic, but the resolution of the first foot suggests a fourth paeon ($\smile\smile\smile\perp$). The thought is of bloodshed.

The antistrophe deserves attention, because it does not exactly correspond. This may be a sign of textual corruption. If so, it is the only sign; and before trying to emend, we should consider whether the lack of correspondence may not be intentional. That, I believe, is the explanation here.

As before, we proceed from trochaic to Anacreontic. Then instead of:

ἑλέναυς ἕλανδρος ἑλέπτολις ἐκ τῶν ἁβροτίμων
<u>Shift   Ionic a minore</u>

we find (709–10):

<u>ὑμέναιον, ὃς τότ' ἐπέρρεπεν γαμβροῖσιν ἀείδειν.</u>

This is an Aeolian couplet, with overlap of one syllable, and, if Ionic a minore is appropriate to the sense of the first passage, the Aeolian couplet is no less appropriate to the sense of the second: Ὑμὴν ὦ ὑμέναι' Ὑμήν, Ὑμὴν ὦ ὑμέναι' ὦ. It would be easy enough to alter ἐπέρρεπεν into ἐπέρρεπε, but to do so would be to spoil a beautiful effect. And our contention is

[1] This couplet moves slowly, partly because of the division of ἀκ-τὰs, and partly because of the ambiguity of κελσάντων: is it in rising rhythm (–⌣–), like the phrases which precede, or in falling (⌣–⌣), as the sequel shows? Euripides writes, in the same rhythm, ἥξει δὴ Σιμόεντα καὶ δίνας ἀργυροειδεῖς (*I.A.* 751–2, p. 49) and σὺν Ἀγαμέμνονι Τρωίας ἐπὶ Σιμουντίδος ἀκτάς (*El.* 440–1).

supported by a later passage in the same antistrophe (715–6)[1], where the poet forgoes exact correspondence in order to re-echo this Aeolian rhythm:

$$\overline{τἀμπροσθ' \;ἢ\; πολύθρηνον\; αἰῶν'\; ἀμφὶ\; πολιτᾶν}$$

Lastly, the antistrophe ends with the same ominous whisper as the strophe, again coupling the hint of a fourth paeon with the thought of bloodshed:

μέλεον αἷμ' ἀνατλᾶσα.

The second strophe (718–27) begins by taking up this Aeolian rhythm:

$$\underset{\text{Glyconic}}{\overline{ἔθρεψεν\; δὲ\; λέοντος\; ἶνιν\; δόμοις}}\; \underset{\text{Glyconic}}{\overline{ἀγάλακτα\; βού-}}$$

$$\underset{\text{Pherecratic}}{\overline{τας\; ἀνὴρ\; φιλόμαστον,}}$$

The first of these two Glyconics is anaclastic: ἔθρεψεν. We remember how the same device was used by Pindar in his first Olympian (ἄριστον) as an anticipation of Paeonic[2]. We shall see that it has the same function here. Then follow three prosodiacs—their dactylic movement is lively and cheerful:

ἐν βιότου προτελείοις ἄμερον εὐφιλόπαιδα καὶ γεραροῖς ἐπί-
χαρτον.

Then, more slowly, trochaic, with two resolutions suggesting the fourth paeon again:

πολέα δ' ἔσχ' ἐν ἀγκάλαις νεοτρόφου τέκνου δίκαν

And finally we return to the opening subject:

φαιδρωπὸν ποτὶ χεῖρα σαίνοντα γαστρὸς ἀνάγκαις.
Aeolian couplet

The third strophe reintroduces dochmiac (738–48)[3]:

πάραυτα δ' ἐλθεῖν ἐς Ἰλίου πόλιν
λέγοιμ' ἂν φρόνημα μὲν νηνέμου γαλάνας,
ἀκασκαῖον δ' ἄγαλμα πλούτου.

---

[1] 715 τἀμπροσθ' ἢ Headlam: παμπροσθῆ.   [2] p. 73.   [3] 740 δ' add. Porson.

I have analysed the last but one of these phrases as a bacchius followed by two slow dochmiacs. It might be taken equally well as follows:

λέγοιμ' ἂν φρόνημα μὲν νηνέμου γαλάνας

In other words, the phrase contains a hint of falling rhythm (νηνέμου γαλάνας), and by this means we are prepared for the next development:

μαλθακὸν ὀμμάτων βέλος, δηξίθυμον ἔρωτος ἄνθος.
Glyconic — Decasyllable

The decasyllable is introduced for the sake of its weak ending, which anticipates a further change of rhythm:

παρακλίνασ' ἐπέκρανεν δὲ γάμου πικρὰς τελευτάς,
Ionic a minore — Anacreontic
δύσεδρος καὶ δυσόμιλος συμένα Πρῑαμίδαισιν,
Ionic a minore
πομπᾷ Διὸς ξενίου νυμφόκλαυτος Ἐρινύς.
Aeol. tripody — Pherecratic

Ionic a minore for the misery brought about by that fateful wedding, Anacreontic for the bride—Helen. And then, through a shift by anacrusis, we are brought back to our Pherecratic cadence.

The third strophe introduces the climax of the ode (760-6)[1], and again the rhythm is dochmiac:

φιλεῖ δὲ τίκτειν ὕβρις μὲν παλαιὰ νεάζουσαν ἐν κακοῖς βροτῶν
Slow dochmiac — Bacchii — Iambic
ὕβριν τότ' ἢ τόθ' ὅτε τὸ κύριον μόλῃ,
Iambic

These bacchii and iambi hold us in suspense: the resolution ὅτε τὸ κύριον (ᴗᴗᴗ‿ᴗ‿ quick dochmiac) marks an advance and leads directly to the climax:

βαθύσκοτον δαίμονα τίταν ἄμαχον ἀπόλεμον,
Slow dochmiac — 4th paeon — Quick dochmiac (resolved)
ἀνίερον θράσος . . .
Quick dochmiac

---

[1] 763 βαθύσκοτον Maehly. τίταν Heimsoeth: νεαρὰ φάους κότον, δαίμονα τε τὸν,

Rhythm as well as sense drives home the reminiscence:
ἄναγνον ἀνίερον . . . τάλαινα παρακοπά . . . ἀνίερον θράσος.

The climax is over, and the strophe is brought to a close
with the usual cadence:

ἀνίερον θράσος μελαίνας μελάθροισιν ἄτας εἰδομέναν τοκεῦσιν.
　　　　Pherecratic　　　　　　　　　　　Pherecratic

Let us review the development of this dochmiac theme,
which is clearly destined to be the central movement in the
musical design of the play. In the first stasimon, the slow
dochmiac ◡⏤◡⏤◡ was developed out of epitrite with anacrusis;
in the second stasimon it was the leading theme, accompanied
by the other slow dochmiac ◡⏤◡◡⏤. From time to time we
heard suggestions of the fourth paeon (◡◡◡⏤), and this has now,
in the third stasimon, been combined with the slow dochmiac
theme so as to produce a new development—the quick dochmiac ◡◡◡⏤◡⏤. Slow dochmiac has had its climax, and quick
dochmiac has grown out of it: we feel that the climax of quick
dochmiac cannot be long delayed.

It does not, however, come immediately. The fourth stasimon—the last before the crisis of the plot—keeps us in suspense.
Agamemnon has entered the palace, and the conviction is
growing on his faithful adherents that he will not be seen alive
again. They sing in the slow trochaic measure which was
heard in the third stasimon (966–8):

τίπτε μοι τόδ' ἐμπέδως δεῖμα προστατήριον

καρδίας τερασκόπου ποτᾶται;

There can be no doubt about the emotional effect of trochaic
here: the short, slow phrases heighten our sense of sinister
foreboding. Aeschylus is repeating an effect which he had
already used in the Persae (117–8):[1]

ταῦτά μου μελαγχίτων φρὴν ἀμύσσεται φόβῳ.

The first strophe has been analysed in a former chapter[2].

[1] See above p. 89. This rhythm, with its connotation of suspense, is burlesqued
by Euripides in the Cyclops: 608–11 λήψεται τὸν τράχηλον ἐντόνως ὁ καρκίνος τοῦ
ξενδαιτυμόνος· πυρὶ γὰρ τάχα φωσφόρους ὀλεῖ κόρας.　　　　　[2] p. 41.

In the second, we think of the dangers attendant on excessive prosperity, and the rhythm is appropriately Ionic a minore (990–1003)[1]:

μάλα γάρ τοι τᾶς πολλᾶς ὑγιείας ἀκόρεστον
Ionic a minore
τέρμα· νόσος γὰρ ἀεὶ βιοτὰν ὁμότοιχος ἐρείδει
Dactylic, echoed from str. 1
καὶ πότμος εὐθυπορῶν ἀνδρὸς ἔπαισεν ἄφνω
Prosodiacs
δυστυχίας πρὸς ἄφαντον ἔρμα.
Aeolian decasyllable

If only a man will exercise moderation, all will be well:

καὶ τὸ μὲν πρὸ χρημάτων κτησίων ὄκνος βαλὼν
Trochaic, from str. 1
σφενδόνας ἀπ' εὐμέτρου,
οὐκ ἔδυ πρόπας δόμος, πημονᾶς γέμων ἄγαν,
οὐδ' ἐπόντισε σκάφος.

As we think of the happiness of the 'modest competence,' we become almost cheerful[2]:

πολλά τοι δόσις ἐκ Διὸς ἀμφιλαφής τε καὶ ἐξ ἀλόκων ἐπετειᾶν
Dactylic
νῆστιν ὤλεσεν νόσον.
Trochaic

Suddenly, we recall the situation. Again, that whisper of horror at the thought of bloodshed (1004–6)[3]:

τὸ δ' ἐπὶ γᾶν πεσὸν ἅπαξ θανάσιμον προπάροιθ' ἀνδρὸς μέλαν
Fourth paeons
αἷμα....

This is why we heard those fourth paeons in the third stasimon: δι' ἔριν αἱματόεσσαν, μέλεον αἷμ' ἀνατλᾶσα. And from

---

[1] 991 ἀεὶ suppl. Blomfield. 992 βιοτὰν sugg. Wecklein: γείτων. 994 ἄφνω δυστυχίας πρὸς suppl. Headlam.

[2] We are reminded how slow trochaic broke similarly into cheerful dactylic at the mention of Zeus in vv. 170–185: see above pp. 106–107.

[3] 1004 πεσὸν Auratus: πεσόνθ'. 1005 προπάροιθ' h: πρόπαρ.

now on we shall have little respite from this rhythm till we have heard the Furies cry: ἐπὶ δὲ τῷ τεθυμένῳ τόδε μέλος, παραφορά, παρακοπὰ φρενοδαλής.

It is a striking climax, and I suggest that the violation of antistrophic correspondence, to which it owes not a little of its effect, was the work of the poet, not of his mediaeval copyists. Hence to seek to emend v. 990 into conformity with v. 1004, as Headlam and Wecklein have done, is a pity; and when Verrall, more cautiously, observes that "the rhythm of 990, as compared with 1004, is, or appears to be, exceptional and unsatisfactory,"[1] we may reply with some confidence that its unsatisfactoriness is only apparent, while its exceptional character is real and deliberate.

The tragedy is brought to its climax—the murder of Agamemnon—by the prophetic utterances of Cassandra; and the rhythm of that scene is quick dochmiac almost throughout, reaching its culmination as the distracted girl sees the Furies exulting over the downfall of the Atreidae (1101-7):

ἒ ἒ παπαῖ παπαῖ, τί τόδε φαίνεται; ἦ δίκτυόν τί γ' Ἄιδου;
Quick dochmiac   Iambic

ἀλλ' ἄρκυς ἡ ξύνευνος, ἡ ξυναιτία
Iambic

φόνου. στάσις δ' ἀκόρετος γένει κατολολυξάτω
                    Quick dochmiac

θύματος λευσίμου.
Cretic

Agamemnon and Cassandra lie dead. The Elders, still intensely excited, reproach the murderess in the same rhythm (1406-7):

τί κακόν, ὦ γύναι, χθονοτρεφὲς ἐδανὸν ἢ ποτὸν

πασαμένα ῥυτᾶς ἐξ ἁλὸς ὅρμενον . . . .

Clytemnestra, standing over the bodies of her victims, replies

[1] Verrall, *Agamemnon*, p. 234.

undaunted in iambics. The excitement of the Elders begins
to subside, and dochmiac gives place to Aeolian (1449–55)[1]:

φεῦ τίς ἂν ἐν τάχει μὴ περιώδυνος μηδὲ δεμνιοτήρης,
‾‾‾‾‾‾‾‾‾‾‾‾‾‾‾‾‾‾‾‾‾‾‾‾
Aeolian tripodies　　　　　　　　Pherecratic
　　　　　　　　　　　　　　　　Aeolian decasyllable
μόλοι τὸν αἰεὶ φέρουσ᾽ ὁμιλεῖν Μοῖρ᾽ ἀτέλευτον ὕπνον δαμέντος
‾‾‾‾‾‾‾‾‾‾‾‾‾‾‾‾‾‾‾‾‾‾‾‾‾‾‾‾‾‾‾‾‾‾‾‾‾‾
Dochmiacs
φύλακος εὐμενεστάτου καὶ πολέα τλάντος γυναικὸς διαί;
‾‾‾‾‾‾‾‾‾‾‾‾‾‾‾‾‾‾‾‾‾‾‾‾‾‾‾‾‾‾
4th paeon　Slow dochmiac　4th paeon　Cretics
πρὸς γυναικὸς δ᾽ ἀπέφθισεν βίον.
‾‾‾‾‾‾‾‾‾‾‾‾‾
Trochaic

The second strophe (1482–9)[2] is similar in effect:

ἢ μέγαν ἢ μέγαν οἴκοις δαίμονα καὶ βαρύμηνιν αἰνεῖς,
‾‾‾‾‾‾‾‾‾‾‾‾‾‾‾‾‾‾‾‾‾‾‾‾‾‾‾
Prosodiac　　　　　　　Aeolian decasyllable
φεῦ φεῦ κακὸν αἶνον ἀτηρᾶς τύχας ἀκορέστου·
‾‾‾‾‾‾‾‾‾‾‾‾‾‾‾‾‾‾‾‾‾
Pherecratic　　　　　Pherecratic
ἰὼ ἰή, διαὶ Διὸς παναιτίου πανεργέτα·
‾‾‾‾‾‾‾‾‾‾‾‾‾‾‾‾‾‾
Iambic
τί γὰρ βροτοῖς ἄνευ Διὸς τελεῖται;
‾‾‾‾‾‾‾‾‾‾‾‾‾‾
Iambic　　　　　Dochmiac
　　　Pherecratic
τί τῶνδ᾽ οὐ θεόκραντόν ἐστιν;
‾‾‾‾‾‾‾‾‾‾‾
Bacchius

Dochmiac is receding into the background; but it will assert
itself once more before the play is over. "Iphigeneia," cries
Clytemnestra, "was murdered by Agamemnon, and I have
murdered him!" The Elders reply, at first in subdued tones
(1532–8)[3]:

ἀμηχανῶ φροντίδος στερηθεὶς εὐπάλαμον μέριμναν
‾‾‾‾‾‾‾‾‾‾‾‾‾‾‾‾‾‾‾‾‾‾‾
Slow dochmiac　　　　　　　Pherecratic
ὅπα τράπωμαι πίτνοντος οἴκου.
‾‾‾‾‾‾‾‾‾‾‾
Slow dochmiac
δέδοικα δ᾽ ὄμβρου κτύπον δομοσφαλῆ
‾‾‾‾‾‾‾‾‾‾‾‾‾‾‾
Slow dochmiac　　　　Iambic

---

[1] 1451 ὁμιλεῖν Headlam: ἐν ἡμῖν. 1454 πολέα Haupt: πολλά.

[2] 1482 ἢ μέγαν suppl. Headlam.

[3] 1537–8 So Headlam: Δίκᾳ...θήγει...θηγάναις.

τὸν αἱματηρόν· ψεκὰς δὲ λήγει.
Slow dochmiac

Δίκα δ' ἐπ' ἄλλο πρᾶγμα θήγεται βλάβης
Iambic

πρὸς ἄλλαις θηγάναισι Μοῖρα.
Slow dochmiac

Then more emphatically, in the antistrophe:

φέρει φέροντ', ἐκτίνει δ' ὁ καίνων·
μίμνει δὲ μίμνοντος ἐν θρόνῳ Διὸς
παθεῖν τὸν ἔρξαντα· θέσμιον γάρ.

We are moving towards the last climax of the play, when, in the altercation with Aegisthus, the name of Orestes will ring out, in much the same way as the Siegfried motive rings out at the end of *Die Walküre*. The law of vengeance which has destroyed Agamemnon shall destroy Clytemnestra too. Blood calls for blood: the first round in this cycle of sin and punishment is over, the second is about to begin. Surely it is not an accident that at the end of the lyrical portion of the play that slow dochmiac rhythm, which marked the first step towards the musical climax, is revived. Our ears, as well as our sense of drama, are led to expect a similar movement rising to a similar climax. Both will be satisfied in the *Choephoroe*.

* * *

The night is over; and Clytemnestra has had bad dreams. The dead are angry, she fears, and so she sends her serving-maids—captives from the sack of Troy—to her murdered husband's tomb with placatory offerings. They obey her as slave obeys master—by compulsion. Their goodwill is reserved for the Avenger, when he comes.

They step down from the palace-doors dancing to iambic rhythm, largely resolved[1]: they are performing a dirge, rending their veils and beating their breasts.

---

[1] The appropriate rhythm: see p. 88.

Str. 1 (22–31)[1]

ἰαλτὸς ἐκ δόμων ἔβην χοὰς προπομπὸς ὀξύχειρι σὺν κόπῳ.
Iambic _____ Iambic

πρέπει παρῇσι φοινίαις ἀμυγμός / ὄνυχος ἄλοκι νεοτόμῳ·
Iambic _____ Trochaic resolved

δι' αἰῶνος δ' ἰυγμοῖσι βόσκεται κέαρ·
Bacch. Trochaic

λινοφθόροι δ' ὑφασμάτων λακίδες ἔφλαδον ὑπ' ἄλγεσιν
Iambic _____ Iambic

πρόστερνοι στολμοὶ πέπλων ἀγελάστοις
Spondaic

ξυμφοραῖς πεπληγμένων.
Trochaic

Iambic shifts by anacrusis to trochaic. In the middle we hear a suggestion of Paeonic rhythm—a bacchius. Then we return to iambic, and through spondaic to trochaic again.

The second and third strophes develop this suggestion of Paeonic:

Str. 2 (42–52)

(Dochmiac)
τοιάνδε χάριν ἀχάριτον ἀπότροπον κακῶν,
Iambic

ἰὼ γαῖα μαῖα, μωμένα μ' ἰάλλει
Shift _____ Trochaic

(Dochmiac)
δύσθεος γυνά· φοβοῦμαι δ' ἔπος τόδ' ἐκβαλεῖν·
Trochaic _____ Trochaic

τί γὰρ λύτρον πεσόντος αἵματος πέδῳ;
Iambic

ἰὼ πάνοιζυς ἑστία, ἰὼ κατασκαφαὶ δόμων.
Iambic _____ Iambic

ἀνήλιοι βροτοστυγεῖς δνόφοι καλύπτουσι δομους
Iambic _____ Shift[2]

δεσποτῶν θανάτοισι.
Pherecratic

---

[1] 24 παρῇσι Hermann, φοινίαις ἀμυγμός Conington : παρηὶς φοίνισσ' ἀμυγμοῖς.

[2] See above, p. 25.

Str. 3 (64–8)[1]

δι᾽ αἷματ᾽ ἐκποθένθ᾽ ὑπὸ χθονὸς τροφοῦ
_____
Iambic

τίτας φόνος πέπηγεν οὐ διαρρύδαν.
_____
Iambic

αἰανὴς ἄτα διαφέρει νόσου πανάρκους τὸν αἴτιον βρύειν.
_____ _____ _____ _____
Spondaic   Paeon   Dochmiac   Iambic

The epode at the end of the stasimon marks the first climax—slow dochmiac.

Ep. (74–82)[2]

ἐμοὶ δ᾽ (ἀνάγκαν γὰρ ἀμφίπτολιν θεοὶ προσήνεγκαν· ἐκ γὰρ
_____
Dochmiacs

οἴκων
_____
(contd.)

πατρῴων δμῶον ἄγον αἶσαν) δίκαια καὶ μὴ πρέποντ᾽ ἀπ᾽ ἀρχᾶς

βίᾳ φρενῶν αἰνέσαι, πικρὸν στύγος κρατούσῃ.

δακρύω δ᾽ ὑφ᾽ εἱμάτων ματαίοισι δεσπόταν τύχαις, κρυφαίοις
_____ _____
Trochaic   Dochmiac

πένθεσιν παχνουμένη.
_____
Trochaic

At Electra's request, the captives sing a "Paean for the dead." They still use the same resolved iambic, but with it they mingle unmistakable hints of quick dochmiac (152–63)[3]:

ἴετε δάκρυ καναχὲς ὀλόμενον ὀλομένῳ δεσπότᾳ,
_____ _____
Trochaic resolved   4th paeon + Cretic

πρὸς ἔρυμα τόδε κακῶν κεδνῶν τ᾽ ἀπότροπον ἄγος ἀπεύχετον,
_____ _____
Iambic   Iambic

κεχυμένων χοᾶν. κλύε δέ μοι, σέβας,
_____ _____
Quick dochmiac   Quick dochmiac

---

[1] 64 ἐκποθένθ᾽ Schütz: ἔκποθεν. 66–8 So Headlam: διαλγὴς ἄτη διαφέρει τὸν αἴτιον παναρκέτας νόσου βρύειν.

[2] 76 I suggest δμῶον ἄγον provisionally for the unrhythmical δούλιον ἐς ἄγον. 78 ἀπ᾽ ἀρχᾶς Headlam: ἀρχὰς βίου. 79 So Headlam: φερομένων αἰνέσαι, πικρὸν φρενῶν.

[3] 155–6 σέβας, κλῦ᾽ Bamberger: κλύε σέβας. 159 ἴτω τις Bothe: ἰώ τίς. 161 ἔργῳ Headlam: ἐν ἔργῳ βέλη. 162 ἀρῆς Headlam: ᾽Άρης.

κλύ', ὦ δέσποτ', ἐξ ἀμαυρᾶς φρενός. ὀτοτοτοτοτοτοῖ.

Slow dochmiac   Slow dochmiac

ἴτω τις δορυσθενὴς ἀνὴρ ἀναλυτὴρ δόμων Σκυθικά τ' ἐν χεροῖν

Slow dochmiac   Quick dochmiac   Quick dochmiac

παλίντον' ἔργῳ 'πιπάλλων ἀρῆς

Slow dochmiac   Slow dochmiac

σχέδιά τ' αὐτόκωπα νωμῶν βέλη.

Quick dochmiac   Slow dochmiac

That is the first movement in the musical design of the *Choephoroe*: the first stasimon culminated in slow dochmiac, and now we have quick dochmiac. The second movement will repeat these two developments with redoubled effect.

We now come to the central piece in the musical design—the joint prayers of Orestes, Electra and the Trojan captives at the tomb of Agamemnon (305–476). It is a dirge; and, as usual in Greek dirges, the mourners are divided into 'leaders' (οἱ ἐξάρχοντες) and chorus. In the dirge for Hector in the last book of the *Iliad*[1] Andromache, Hecuba and Helen are the leaders, and Trojan women are the chorus:

παρά δ' εἷσαν ἀοιδοὺς

θρήνων ἐξάρχους, οἵ τε στονόεσσαν ἀοιδὴν

οἱ μὲν δὴ θρήνεον, ἐπὶ δὲ στενάχοντο γυναῖκες[2].

The Homeric dirge is arranged as follows:

Andromache: Hector (thrice)

  ἐπὶ δὲ στενάχοντο γυναῖκες (*Chorus*).

Hecuba: Hector!

  γόον δ' ἀλίαστον ὄρινε (*Chorus*).

Helen: Hector!

  ἐπὶ δὲ στένε δῆμος ἀπείρων (*Chorus*).

The arrangement of the Aeschylean dirge is rather more elaborate. The leaders are only two—Orestes and Electra.

Anapaests: Δίκη μέγ' ἀυτεῖ.

Or. O Father.

Cho. The dead.

El. O Father.

---

[1] Hom. *Il.* xxiv, 718–76.   [2] *Ibid.* 720–2.

Anapaests: παιὰν ἐν μελάθροις.
Or. Troy.
Cho. The dead.
El. Troy.
Anapaests: διπλῆς μαράγνης δοῦπος ἱκνεῖται.
Or. Zeus.
Cho. Revenge!
El. Zeus.
Anapaests: βοᾷ λοιγὸς Ἐρινύν.
Or. The survivors of the house.
Cho. Apprehension.
El. Sufferings of the survivors.
Cho. Renewal of dirge.
El. A.'s dishonoured burial.
Or. Revenge!
Cho. Mutilation of the body.
El. My own sufferings.
Or. El. Cho. O Father!
Or. El. Cho. Δίκη.
Cho. Apprehension.

The brother and sister begin by lamenting their father's
death: the Trojan women urge them to pray also for revenge.
They obey, but now the Trojans begin to lose heart, disquieted
by fears for the future (409-13). Reminding themselves, however, of the horror of Clytemnestra's crime, they renew the
dirge with added vigour (422-7), and the same thought drives
Orestes and Electra to pray still more passionately for revenge.
The fears of the Chorus return, and finally, overcome with apprehension, they drop out altogether, leaving brother and sister
to finish their invocation in iambic dialogue.

Thus the poem falls into two parts. In the first (305-421)
the Chorus take the lead, in the second (422-76) they lose
confidence. In the first, the brother and sister are slow in
framing the vengeful prayer which the Trojan women dictate

to them, in the second they pray for vengeance with the greatest vehemence.

Orestes begins the invocation, gently, in Aeolian:

Str. 1 (314–21)[1]

ὦ πάτερ αἰνόπατερ, τί σοι φάμενος ἢ τί ῥέξας

<u>Aeolian enneasyllable</u>   <u>Pherecratic</u>

τύχοιμ᾽ ἂν τόθεν οὐρίσας, ἔνθα σ᾽ ἔχουσιν εὐναί;

<u>Anacl. Glyconic</u>   <u>Pherecratic</u>

σκότῳ φάος ἀντίμοιρον· χάριτες δ᾽ ὁμοίως

<u>Pherecratic with anacr.</u>   <u>Echo</u>

κέκληνται γόος εὐκλεὴς προσθοδόμοις Ἀτρείδαις.

<u>Anacl. Glyconic</u>   <u>Pherecratic</u>

The shift to rising rhythm in the middle (χάριτες δ᾽ ὁμοίως) anticipates the movement of the second strophe, which introduces Anacreontic—a rhythm associated, like the kindred Ionic a minore, with lamentation[2]:

Str. 2 (322–30)

τέκνον, φρόνημα τοῦ θανόντος οὐ δαμάζει

<u>Iambic</u>   <u>Iambic</u>

πυρὸς μαλερὰ γνάθος, φαίνει δ᾽ ὕστερον ὀργάς·

<u>Shift</u>   <u>Pherecratic</u>

ὀτοτύζεται δ᾽ ὁ θνῄσκων, ἀναφαίνεται δ᾽ ὁ βλάπτων.

<u>Anacreontic</u>   <u>Anacreontic</u>

πατέρων τε καὶ τεκόντων γόος ἔνδικος ματεύει

<u>Anacreontic</u>   <u>Anacreontic</u>

<u>Shift</u>

τὸ πᾶν ἀμφιλαφὴς ταραχθείς.

<u>Pherecratic</u>

Notice how the shift from rising rhythm back to Pherecratic is made an opportunity of introducing a touch of Paeonic. This is developed in the third strophe, which, while still mainly Aeolian, introduces slow dochmiac:

---

[1] 316 ἂν τόθεν or σ᾽ ἔκαθεν Headlam: ἂν ἔκαθεν.

[2] For Anacreontic with the idea of lamentation, cf. Aesch. *P. V.* 413–21, Soph. *Phil.* 1176–7, Eur. *Alc.* 398. It is a recurrent theme in the *Philoctetes* (136, 687–90, 711, 856, 1140, 1145, 1176–7): cf. *Ant.* 583, 622, 791–2, 839–40.

126 GREEK LYRIC METRE

Str. 3 (344–52)[1]

εἰ γὰρ ὑπ' Ἰλίῳ πρός τινος Λυκίων, πάτερ,
(A) Aeol. tripody   Glyconic

δορίτμητος κατηναρίσθης, λιπὼν ἂν εὔκλειαν ἐν δόμοισιν
Slow dochmiac   Slow dochmiac

τέκνων τ' ἐν κελεύθοις ἐπίστρεπτον αἰῶ
Bacchii

κτίσας πολύχωστον ἂν εἶχες τάφον διαποντίου γᾶς
Dactylic with anacrusis   (A) Pherecratic with anacr.

δώμασιν εὐφόρητον.
Pherecratic

Orestes appeals to Zeus. Accordingly, his Aeolian is mixed with prosodiac, anticipated by the dactylic phrase in the last strophe:

Str. 4 (379–84)[2]

τοῦτο διαμπερέως ἵκεθ' ἅπερ τι βέλος. Ζεῦ, Ζεῦ κάτωθεν ἰάλλων
Prosodiac   Prosodiac   Pherecratic

ὑστερόποινον ἄταν
Pherecratic
Bacchius

βροτῶν τλήμονι καὶ πανούργῳ χειρὶ τοκεῦσι δ' ὅμως τελεῖται.
Pherecratic   Decasyllable

In the fifth strophe the excitement of the captives is at its height, as is indicated by the abrupt changes of rhythm and by a touch of choriambic:

Str. 5 (385–92)[3]

ἐφυμνῆσαι γένοιτό μοι πευκήεντ' ὀλολυγμὸν ἀνδρὸς
Dochmiac   Aeolian decasyllable

θεινομένου, γυναικός τ' ὀλλυμένας· τί γὰρ κεύ-
Pherecratic   Pherecratic

θω φρέν' ὃ σεῖον ἔμπας ποτᾶται; πάροιθεν δὲ πρῴρας
Pherecratic   Bacchii

δριμὺς ἄηται κραδίας θυμός, ἔγκοτον στύγος.
Choriambic   Trochaic

[1] 350 κτίσας Headlam : κτίσσας.
[2] 379 διαμπερέως Headlam : διαμπερὲς οὖς. 381 ἰάλλων Emperius : ἀμπέμπων.
[3] 389 φρέν' ὃ σεῖον Headlam : φρενὸς θεῖον.

Orestes now takes the lead, and develops the dochmiac theme introduced in the third strophe:

Str. 6 (404–8)[1]

ποποῖ δᾶ, νερτέρων τυραννίδες
Slow dochmiac
ἴδετε πολυκρατεῖς ἀραὶ τεθυμένων,
Quick dochmiac
ἴδεσθ᾽ Ἀτρειδᾶν τὰ λοίπ᾽ ἀμηχάνως
Slow dochmiac
ἔχοντα καὶ δωμάτων ἄτιμα. πᾷ τις τράποιτ᾽ ἄν, ὦ Ζεῦ;
Slow dochmiac

With this dochmiac climax the first part of the invocation comes to an end. The Chorus resumes the dirge in resolved iambic with an admixture of Paeonic (422–7); and with the next utterance of Orestes slow dochmiac returns, now more insistent than ever:

Str. 8 (433–7)

τὸ πᾶν ἀτίμως ἔλεξας; οἴμοι. πατρὸς δ᾽ ἀτίμωσιν ἆρα τίσει
Slow dochmiacs
ἕκατι μὲν δαιμόνων, ἕκατι δ᾽ ἁμᾶν χερῶν.
Slow dochmiacs
ἔπειτ᾽ ἐγὼ νοσφίσας ὀλοίμαν.
Slow dochmiacs

And the same rhythm is maintained till we reach the climax of the dirge. Brother and sister are crying out for their mother's blood:

Str. 9 (454–8)

Ὀρ. σέ τοι λέγω, ξυγγενοῦ, πάτερ, φίλοις.

Ἠλ. ἐγὼ δ᾽ ἐπιφθέγγομαι κεκλαυμένα.

Χο. στάσις δὲ πάγκοινος ἅδ᾽ ἐπιρροθεῖ,

ἄκουσον ἐς φάος μολών, ξὺν δὲ γενοῦ πρὸς ἐχθρούς.
Iambic   Pherecratic

That last Pherecratic—we have not heard this phrase in the

[1] 404 ποποῖ δᾶ Headlam: ποῖ ποῖ δή. 405 τεθυμένων Hermann: φθιμένων.

last three strophes—brings us to the conclusion. The Trojan captives are no longer inciting their masters to pray for vengeance, they are weeping for the sorrows of the house of Atreus, past, present and to come, and return to the Aeolian rhythms with which the scene began:

Str. 10 (464–8)

ὦ πόνος ἐγγενὴς καὶ παράμουσος ἄτης αἱματόεσσα πλαγά.
Aeolian tripody   Pherecratic   Pherecratic

ἰὼ δύστον' ἄφερτα κήδη· ἰὼ δυσκατάπαυστον ἄλγος.
    Pherecratic   Pherecratic

There are two more stasima before the crisis of the play, and both are composed mainly in that trochaic rhythm which was used for the same purpose in the *Agamemnon* (686 and 966). The first (583–648) contains four strophes: strophe 1 has trochaic and dactylic for its two subjects, and they are arranged in the same manner as *Agamemnon* 170–85 (A–B–A); strophe 2 introduces Aeolian; and strophes 3 and 4 bring us back to slow dochmiac. The second (779–836) marks a further advance. Orestes has entered the palace, the hour of vengeance is come, and the Trojan captives pray that his enterprise may prosper.

Str. 1 (779–84)[1]

νῦν παραιτουμένᾳ μοι, πάτερ Ζεῦ θεῶν Ὀλυμπίων,
(A) Cretic   Trochaic

δὸς τύχας· τυχεῖν δέ μου κυρίως τὸ σωφρονεῖν
Trochaic   Trochaic

μαιομένοις ἰδεῖν. διὰ δίκας πᾶν ἔπος/ἔλακον. ὦ
(B) Quick dochm.   4th paeon   Cretic   4th paeon

Ζεῦ, σύ νιν φυλάσσοις.
(A) Trochaic

Then follows a refrain in which the captives continue their prayer in Ionic a minore—the rhythm of lamentation,—and in

---

[1] 782 τὸ σωφρονεῖν Headlam: τὰ σωφροσύνην. 783 διὰ δίκας Pauw: διαδικᾶσαι. 784 ἔλακον. ὦ Ζεῦ, σύ νιν Hermann: ἔλακον. Ζεῦ, σὺ δέ νιν.

quick dochmiac—the rhythm which the *Agamemnon* has taught
us to associate with bloodshed, and its price—suffering.

ἐ ἔ. πρὸ δὲ δὴ 'χθρῶν τὸν ἔσωθεν μελάθρων, Ζεῦ,
<u>Ionic a minore</u>
θές, ἐπεί νιν μέγαν ἄρας, δίδυμα καὶ τριπλᾶ
<u>Ionic a minore</u>   <u>Quick paeonic</u>
παλίμποινα θέλων ἀμείψει.
<u>Pherecratic</u>

"And thou shalt exact payment twice, yea thrice over." From
Clytemnestra? or from Orestes?

The captives have forgotten, in the excitement of the moment, the fears for the future they expressed at the end of the
invocation of the dead; but the rhythm in which they sing
prevents the audience from forgetting. The refrain appended
to the second strophe is no less significant (802–7)[1]:

<u>Pherecratic</u>
τὸ δὲ καλῶς κτίμενον ὦ μέγα ναίων
<u>4th paeon</u>   <u>4th paeon</u>
στόμιον, εὖ δὸς ἀναδεῖν δόμον ἀνδρός,
καί νιν ἐλευθερίως λαμπρὸν ἰδεῖν φιλίοις
<u>Dactylic</u>   <u>Dactylic</u>
ὄμμασιν ἐκ δνοφερᾶς καλύπτρας.
<u>Aeolian decasyllable</u>

Could anything be more untimely than the cheerfulness of those
light dactylic and Aeolian phrases? Aeschylus is here strongly
contrasting rhythm with sense—for dramatic effect.

The cries of Aegisthus are heard as Orestes puts him to death.
Clytemnestra comes to the palace-door in alarm. Orestes follows her, and rejecting his mother's appeal for mercy drives
her to her fate.

The Trojan captives are overjoyed, and they utter a cry of
Alleluia! But they sing to the music of the Furies (934–7),

---

[1] 804 ἀναδεῖν Headlam: ἀνιδεῖν. 806 λαμπρὸν Ahrens: λαμπρῶς. 807 ὄμμασιν ἐκ
Hermann: ὄμμασι.

T   9

just as Siegfried and Brünnhilde, all unconsciously, sing of their happiness to the tune of the curse which overhangs them:

ἔμολε μὲν Δίκα Πριαμίδαις χρόνῳ, βαρύδικος Ποινά·
ἔμολε δ' ἐς δόμον τὸν Ἀγαμέμνονος διπλοῦς λέων, διπλοῦς Ἄρης.

Here at last we have the theme of the Avengers of blood-shed—the rhythm which accompanied the wild utterances of Cassandra as she saw the fearful revellers at their feast. "Justice came in time to Priam, even so has Orestes brought justice to the house of Agamemnon." Therefore (941–4):

ἐπολολύξατ' ὦ δεσποσύνων δόμων
ἀναφυγὰς κακῶν καὶ κτεάνων τριβᾶς
ὑπὸ δυοῖν μιαστόροιν, δυσοίμου τύχας.

Our analogy between the first and second plays of the trilogy is now complete: the musical structure of both has culminated in the rhythm which Aeschylus has consecrated to the unseen Avengers, who have made, then Clytemnestra, now Orestes, their instruments. In the third play of the trilogy these terrible divinities will appear before our eyes, and will themselves chant the fatal song which casts the spell of madness over their unhappy victim.

Awoken by the shade of Clytemnestra, one·by one the Furies rise and step out of the semi-darkness of Apollo's shrine into the light of day. The rhythm is what we expect it to be (143–6):

ἰοὺ ἰού, πύπαξ. ἐπάθομεν, φίλαι,   . . .
ἐπάθομεν πάθος δυσαχές, ὦ πόποι,
ἄφερτον κακόν.

They begin their binding-song slowly in cretic and heavily protracted trochaic (322–8)[1]. Then comes the refrain—the magic spell (329–34):

ἐπὶ δὲ τῷ τεθυμένῳ τόδε μέλος, παρακοπά, παραφορὰ φρενοδαλής

---

[1] See above, p. 16.

The music of the *Agamemnon* echoes in our ears (1004–5):

τὸ δ' ἐπὶ γᾶν πεσὸν ἅπαξ θανάσιμον προπάροιθ' ἀνδρὸς μέλαν αἷμα . . .

Thus, the rhythm which marked the climax of the *Agamemnon* and the *Choephoroe* now marks the climax of the whole trilogy—the most tremendous scene in Greek tragedy; it created a panic in the theatre at the time, and was remembered long afterwards. When Sophocles and Euripides wished to allude to this episode in their own versions of the legend, they wisely refrained from attempting new effects, and contented themselves with recalling the old:

Soph. *El.* 1384–8

ἴδεθ' ὅπου προνέμεται τὸ δυσέριστον αἷμα φυσῶν Ἄρης.
βεβᾶσιν ἄρτι δωμάτων ὑπόστεγοι
μετάδρομοι κακῶν πανουργημάτων ἄφυκτοι κύνες.

Eur. *Or.* 316–23

αἰαῖ, δρομάδες ὦ πτεροφόροι ποτνιάδες θεαί,
ἀβάκχευτον αἳ θίασον ἐλάχετ' ἐν δάκρυσι καὶ γόοις,
μελάγχρωτες εὐμενίδες, αἵτε τὸν
ταναὸν αἰθέρ' ἀμπάλλεσθ', αἵματος
τινύμεναι δίκαν, τινύμεναι φόνον . . .

The dominant rhythm of the third stasimon is trochaic (493–568); and here again the *Eumenides* closely follows the two preceding plays. This is the rhythm used by the Argive elders to express their foreboding of Clytemnestra's vengeance, and by the Trojan captives as they awaited the vengeance of Orestes. Now we hear it a third time as the Furies await the verdict which is to decide whether or no they may take vengeance on Orestes.

Before the stasimon ends, slow dochmiac creeps in again (553–5):

ἑκὼν δ' ἀνάγκας ἄτερ δίκαιος ὢν οὐκ ἄνολβος ἔσται·
πανώλεθρος δ' οὔποτ' ἂν γένοιτο.

To what climax does it lead now? To the threat of the Furies that they will lay a heavy hand on the city which has dishonoured them; and as that threat is uttered, we hear the fourth paeon and a touch of quick dochmiac for the last time (783–96)[1]:

ἐγὼ δ' ἄτιμος ἡ τάλαινα βαρύκοτος
ἐν γᾷ τᾷδε, φεῦ,
ἰὸν ἰὸν ἀντιπενθῆ μεθεῖσα καρδίας σταλαγμὸν
χθονὶ ἄφορον· ἐκ δὲ τοῦ λειχὴν ἄφυλλος ἄτεκνος,
ἰὼ Δίκα, πέδον ἐπισύμενος
βροτοφθόρους κηλῖδας ἐν χώρᾳ βαλεῖ.
στενάζω; τί ῥέξω; γένωμαι δυσοίστα πολίταις;
ἔπαθον ὦ μεγάλα τοι Κόραι δυστυχεῖς Νυκτὸς ἀτιμοπενθεῖς.

Pherecratic

And yet again, a little later (840–3):

ἐμὲ παθεῖν τάδε, φεῦ, ἐμὲ παλαιόφρονα, κατά τε γᾶν οἰκεῖν
ἀτίετον, φεῦ μύσος. πνέω τοι μένος ἅπαντά τε κότον.

Happily, their threat is not carried out. Instead, they accept the friendship of Athena and the honours of her beloved city. They are escorted to their new homes by a band of Athenian citizens, and for the last time we hear the cry of Alleluia!

ὀλολύξατε νῦν ἐπὶ μολπαῖς.

The full musical beauty of the *Oresteia* has perished beyond recall. However closely we may study the rhythm, the melody still eludes us. The fruit has withered, and we are left with the husk. But we can get a good deal of pleasure, even out of the husk.

---

[1] 794 ὦ: ἰώ.

SUPPLEMENTARY NOTES.

1. Aeschylus, *Prometheus Vinctus.*

The lyrical design of this play is very simple—rather Sophoclean in manner,—compared with that of *The Supplices* or the *Oresteia.* There are five musical scenes—a parodos, a monody, and three short stasima. The leading theme of the parodos and of the first stasimon is the Anacreontic, while the last two stasima are in Dorian rhythm. This change of subject reflects a change in the attitude of the Oceanids towards Prometheus. At first, they are more compassionate than remonstrative—hence the Anacreontics of the parodos (130–60) and the Anacreontics and Ionics a minore of the first stasimon (413–30). But they also feel that Prometheus has sinned against the virtue of moderation in transgressing the will of Zeus—hence the solemn Dorian of the second stasimon (542–80). The subject of the third stasimon (913–38) is the wisdom of moderation in marriage, again in Dorian—the rhythm used by Euripides, we remember, for the same subject in the *Medea* (627–41, p. 48). Besides these two motives, we must notice the development of a third—Paeonic. It appears first in the soliloquy of Prometheus: 115–6 τίς ἀχώ, τίς ὀδμὰ προσέπτα μ᾽ ἀφεγγής; 118 ἵκετο τερμόνιον ἐπὶ πάγον. It reappears under cover of the resolved iambics of the parodos (170 ἐπιχαρῆ, 173 ἐπικότως ἀεί), and again in the epode appended to the first stasimon: 441–9 μόνον δὴ πρόσθεν ἄλλον ἐν πόνοις ... Τιτᾶνα λύμαις ἐσιδόμαν θεόν ... κελαινὸς δ᾽ Ἄϊδος ὑποβρέμει μυχός. This motive reaches its consummation in the continuous Paeonic of the monody of Io (588–635).

174 θέμενος ἄγναμπτον νόον: two epitrites (see p. 23). The corresponding phrase in the antistrophe is plain iambic: 196 δέδια γὰρ ἀμφὶ σαῖς τύχαις. But perhaps we should read δέδια δ᾽ (Triclinius), the γὰρ having originated in the common gloss ὁ δέ ἀντὶ τοῦ γάρ; cf. schol. in 556, and schol. Eur. *Or.* 36;

Aesch. *Agam*. 425 εὐμόρφων δὲ vulg. εὐμόρφων γὰρ h. This strophe is bound to the preceding by the cadence: 179 = 135, cf. 140.

436. Note the resolution in anticipation of Paeonic (◡◡◡ – ◡⊥◡⊥–).

542–80. The first strophe is pure Dorian, the second begins in rising rhythm for the sake of a passing allusion to Anacreontic: 561-3 φέρ' ὅπως χάρις ἁ χάρις· ὦ φίλος, εἰπὲ ποῦ τις ἀλκά; ·571-3 ἔμαθον τάδε σὰς προσιδοῦσ' ὀλοὰς τύχας, Προμηθεῦ—a clear reminiscence of 413-14 στένω σε τᾶς οὐλομένας τύχας, Προμηθεῦ. Anacreontic will recur once again: 721 πέφρικ' ἐσιδοῦσα πρᾶξιν Ἰοῦς. 559 ἰδίᾳ is corrupt. The original reading was perhaps οἰκείᾳ (Tricl.), glossed by ἰδίᾳ (which crept into the text) and by αὐθαιρέτῳ (gl. rec.) to show that the word is used here in its sense of *proprius*, not *propinquus*: cf. *Cho.* 671 οἰκείᾳ σάγῃ· ἐπὶ ἰδίᾳ πραγματείᾳ schol., Hesych. οἰκεῖοι· οἱ κατ' ἐπιγαμίαν ἀλλήλοις προσήκοντες· ἢ ἴδιοι. For the shortening of the diphthong before the vowel cf. *Theb.* 710 εὐκταίαν, Anacr. 1, 4 Ληθαίου, Soph. *El.* 849 δειλαία δειλαίων, 1058 οἰωνούς, *Ajax* 1190 Τροίαν, *O. C.* 118 ναίει, *Ant.* 1307 ἀνταίαν, Eur. *H. F.* 409 Μαιῶτιν, Bacchyl. xvi 129 παιάνιξαν.

2. Sophocles, *Antigone*.

The regular accompaniment of the tragic crisis in the plays of Sophocles and Euripides is Paeonic, after the example set by Aeschylus in *The Suppliants* and the *Oresteia*. In the *Antigone* we have a good example of the way in which the Paeonic climax is built up.

The parodos begins in Aeolian (100–27):

Glyconic   Glyconic
ἀκτὶς ἀελίου, τὸ κάλλιστον ἑπταπύλῳ φανὲν

Glyconic   Anacl. Glyconic
Θήβᾳ τῶν πρότερον φάος, ἐφάνθης ποτ', ὦ χρυσέας

Tripody   Glyconic
ἀμέρας βλέφαρον, Διρκαίων ὑπὲρ ῥεέθρων μολοῦσα . . .
                    Pherecratic

Observe how the words are grouped (always important in Sophocles: the divisions are the same in the antistrophe): ἀκτὶς ἀελίου suggests ἀμέρας βλέφαρον, τὸ κάλλιστον ἑπταπύλῳ suggests ἐφάνθης ποτ', ὦ χρυσέας, while ὦ χρυσέας anticipates the choriambic movement in the next strophe. Further, in τὸ κάλλιστον, and still more in ἐφάνθης ποτ', ὦ, do we not hear an intimation of rising rhythm—Paeonic?

The first stasimon begins in the same Aeolian rhythm (332–41):

Glyconic	Glyconic

πολλὰ τὰ δεινά, κοὐδὲν ἀνθρώπου δεινότερον πέλει . . .

In the body of the strophe there is a touch of iambic, then a dactylic phrase (see p. 23), and finally the following close: ἱππείῳ γένει πολεύων. The dactyls we have just heard incline us to take this phrase as trochaic; at the same time we can hardly fail to recognise in ἱππείῳ an echo of ἀνθρώπου. This leaves us with γένει πολεύων—a dochmiac. After this, we shall not be surprised to hear in the next strophe, following three prosodiacs (derived from the dactyls of the first strophe): δυσαύλων πάγων ὑπαίθρεια καὶ δύσομβρα φεύγειν βέλη.

The second stasimon (583–625) begins in Dorian. Now we know why we had those prosodiacs in the last stasimon: 583 εὐδαίμονες οἶσι κακῶν repeats 354 καὶ φθέγμα καὶ ἀνέμοεν. But again notice the division of the words:

Prosodiac	Epitrite

εὐδαίμονες οἶσι κακῶν ἄγευστος αἰών
Dochmiac

Accordingly, at the end of the strophe we hear: 590 κυλίνδει βυσσόθεν κελαινάν.

The third stasimon (781–801) is the hymn to Eros: Dorian gives place to Aeolian, and dochmiac is temporarily discarded. In the antistrophe (not in the strophe) the words are grouped so as to suggest Anacreontic: 791–2 σὺ καὶ δικαίων ἀδίκους φρένας παρασπᾷς. This is in anticipation of the lyrical lament

which follows. Is it also a reminiscence of 622 τὸ κακὸν
δοκεῖν ποτ' ἐσθλόν?

Anacl. Glyconic	Anacl. Pherecratic	Pherecratic with
Ἔρως ἀνίκατε μάχαν,	Ἔρως ὃς ἐν κτήνεσι πίπτεις,	ὃς ἐν μαλακαῖς
Iambo-choriambic	Iambo-choriambic	
anacrusis Repeat		

παρειαῖς νεάνιδος ἐννυχεύεις . . .

Here Aeolian runs against iambo-choriambic. In the next
strophe (806) this effect is repeated:

Iambo-choriambic
ὁρᾶτ' ἔμ', ὦ γᾶς πατρίας πολῖται
Pherecratic

Then Aeolian is abandoned, giving place to Anacreontic
(839–40):

Iambo-choriambic
οἴμοι γελῶμαι. τί με πρὸς θεῶν πατρῴων . . .
Anacreontic

In ὁρᾶτ' ἔμ', ὦ γᾶς, and still more clearly in οἴμοι γελῶμαι, we
hear dochmiac. And so, before long, we get (852) μέτοικος,
οὐ ζῶσιν, οὐ θανοῦσιν and (856) πατρῷον δ' ἐκτίνεις τιν' ἆθλον.
The fourth stasimon (944–87) resumes the Dorian motive,
but those sinister dochmiacs are becoming more insistent than
ever: 954 κελαιναὶ νᾶες ἐκφύγοιεν, 973–6 τυφλωθὲν ἐξ ἀγρίας
δάμαρτος . . . ἀραχθέντων ὑφ' αἱματηραῖς χείρεσσι καὶ κερκίδων
ἀκμαῖσιν. Finally, after a short stasimon which begins with
an echo of 583 (1116 πολυώνυμε Καδμείας ἄγαλμα νύμφας)
the Paeonic climax is at last released: 1261 f. ἰὼ φρενῶν
δυσφρόνων ἁμαρτήματα στερεὰ θανατόεντ' . . .

3. Sophocles, Ajax.

Here there are two Paeonic pieces—the first for the scene
(348–428) in which Ajax determines to die (cf. 394–6 ἰὼ σκότος
ἐμὸν φάος, ἔρεβος ὦ φαεννότατον ὡς ἐμοί, ἕλεσθ' ἕλεσθέ μ' οἰκή-
τορα), and the second for the scene (866–960) in which his
dead body is discovered (cf. 925–8 ἔμελλες τάλας ἔμελλες
χρόνῳ στερεόφρων ἄρ' ἐξανύσσειν κακὰν μοῖραν ἀπειρεσίων

πόνων). The other odes are grouped around these two scenes. The first stasimon (172–256) begins in Dorian.—The epitrites ψευσθεῖσ᾽ ἀδώροις...ἢ χαλκοθώραξ (178–9) lead, in the second strophe, to 227 οἴμοι φοβοῦμαι and 245 ὥρα τιν᾽ ἤδη, in anticipation of dochmiac. The first Paeonic scene contains touches of Aeolian: 399 οὔθ᾽ ἀμερίων ἔτ᾽ ἄξιος, 408–9 ἄν με χειρὶ φονεύοι. We are thus prepared for the next stasimon (596–645) in which the sailors sing of their longing for Salamis and for rest from war in Aeolian (pp. 63 and 24). Dochmiac is heard in 600 ἐγὼ δ᾽ ὁ τλάμων, 601 μίμνων ἀν᾽ Ἴδαν, 624 ἦ που παλαιᾷ, 625 λευκῷ τε γήρᾳ, 634 ἄμυγμα χαίτας. Notice also πολιᾶς ἄμυγμα χαίτας—an Anacreontic. In the next stasimon (693–718) despondency gives way to gaiety: dochmiac disappears (except perhaps for 705 ἐμοὶ ξυνείη), and Glyconic is combined with Anacreontic (pp. 31–2). But this misplaced confidence only serves to heighten the tragic effect of the next scene—the second Paeonic climax. There is one more stasimon (1185–1202), which brings us back to the ode to Salamis, both in thought—longing for peace and home, and in rhythm—Aeolian:

Glyconic   Pherecratic
——————————————   ——————————
τίς ἄρα νέατος ἔς ποτε λήξει πολυπλάγκτων ἐτέων ἀριθμός;
              Choriambic

And again at the end (1217–22: p. 63), Aeolian provides an appropriate accompaniment to the mention of holy Athens.

Peace after suffering—a peace won only by the wisdom of the servant of Athena: that is the consummation effected in the last scene of the *Ajax*. Is not this consummation beautifully anticipated in the last movement of the music?

4. Sophocles, *Electra*.

This play, which is later than the *Antigone* and *Ajax*, is marked by certain departures from the Aeschylean tradition, both in phrasing and in composition. Nevertheless, though latent, the old principles are still at work.

First of all we have the parodos (121–250), the main subjects of which are the following: (1) spondaic, passing readily into anapaestic; (2) the dactylic tetrapody, usually in pairs (124–5, 130–3, 166–70, 236–7); (3) ⌣⌣⌣⌣⌣⌣ (a rhythm not easy to classify: see Appendix) in various combinations (156, 160–3, 207, 209–10, 212); (4) Aeolian (tripodies 205, 243–5; Glyconic 248; Pherecratic 232?); (5) dochmiac. The form of the composition as a whole is defined by the dochmiac cadences: thus the figure ⌣⌣⌣⌣ ⌣⌣⌣⌣ occurs thrice—at the end of the first part of str. 1 (128 ὄλοιτ᾽ εἴ μοι θέμις τόδ᾽ αὐδᾶν), at the end of str. 2 (172 ποθῶν δ᾽ οὐκ ἀξιοῖ φανῆναι), and finally at the end of the epode (250 ἀπάντων τ᾽ εὐσέβεια θνατῶν) which is further emphasised by a repetition from the close of str. 1 (249 ἔρροι τ᾽ ἂν αἰδώς repeats 136 αἰαῖ ἱκνοῦμαι). Similarly, in str. 1 the dochmiac close (135–6) answers the dochmiac already heard in 128, in str. 2 171–2 answers 155 and 159. The ⌣⌣⌣⌣ motive accompanies the first mention of the Avenger, Orestes (160–3 ὄλβιος, ὃν ἁ κλεινὰ γᾶ ποτε Μυκηναίων δέξεται εὐπατρίδαν, Διὸς εὔφρονι βήματι μολόντα τάνδε γᾶν Ὀρέσταν), and is again associated with Orestes in the corresponding part of the antistrophe (180–4 οὔτε γὰρ ὁ τὰν Κρίσᾳ βούνομον ἔχων ἀκτὰν παῖς Ἀγαμεμνονίδας ἀπερίτροπος). In 209–10 οἷς θεὸς ὁ μέγας Ὀλύμπιος ποίνιμα πάθεα παθεῖν πόροι, the same rhythm marks an appeal to Zeus for vengeance. It will be heard again at the end of the first stasimon (504–15) in the description of the fatal race of Pelops (an apt prelude to the race of Orestes, which is not the less ominous because it is fictitious) and yet again in the renewed appeal to Zeus at the beginning of the next stasimon (823 ποῦ ποτε κεραυνοὶ Διός...). Clearly, the motive has a dramatic significance: Sophocles has not departed from the practice of his predecessor so far as to abandon the leit-motive.

The first stasimon (473–515) begins in choriambic (for prophecy, p. 59). Then we get some trochaic and iambic phrases and a Pherecratic: in 479 and 495 read θράσος, not θάρσος. Then comes a long phrase (repeated) not found in Aeschylus (482–5):

οὐ γάρ ποτ' ἀμναστεῖ γ' ὁ φύσας σ' Ἑλλάνων ἄναξ,
οὐδ' ἁ παλαιὰ χαλκόπλακτος ἀμφάκης γένυς.

The first figure seems to be based on the epitrite, while the second (ἀμφάκης γένυς) seems to be derived from the Aeolian tripody heard at the end of the choriambics above: λειπομένα σοφᾶς. Then, finally, we get another Pherecratic and a protracted epitrite:

ἅ νιν κατέπεφνεν αἰσχίσταις ἐν αἰκείαις.

The epode reintroduces the ⏓∪∪∪⏓ motive already noticed, and with it ∪∪∪∪ ⏓–⏓ (πολύπονος ἱππεία—equivalent to εἰ μὴ 'γὼ παράφρων=ἥξει καὶ πολύπους), two spondaic figures (510–11), and a touch of cretic (507, 513).

In the next stasimon (823–70) the initial allusion to the ⏓∪∪∪⏓ motive passes, through a resumption of choriambic, into Ionic a minore. The second strophe reintroduces spondaic (850–2) and dochmiac (855 παραγάγῃς ἵν' οὔ). The third stasimon (1058–97) is in concurrent iambo-choriambic and Anacreontic, with an Aeolian centre (pp. 31, 29). The second strophe (Dorian, with iambic) brings us back to dochmiac: 1083 κακῶς εὔκλειαν αἰσχῦναι θέλει, 1089 σοφά τ' ἀρίστα τε παῖς κεκλῆσθαι. Then comes the ἀναγνώρισις (1232–87), passionate and tragic, in Paeonic, which leads directly to the tragic crisis (1384–1441), again in Paeonic.

5. Pindar.

The following notes, supplementing the account I have already given in Chapters V and VII, may be of use to the reader who wishes to study some of the more difficult Pindaric Odes. It will be seen that in many of them the poet discards the conventional phrasing of the early lyrical tradition, and that his formal design, so far as it depends on the rhythm, is often implicit and allusive, being based upon echo and reminiscence rather than upon the formal arrangement of definite themes. This is just what we should expect: as soon as an artistic convention has become established, the progressive artist tends to work away from it.

N. vi.   Triadic : Paeonic, Aeolian and Dorian.
Str.

Bacchius   Glyconic   Paeon

ἐν ἀνδρῶν, ἔν θεῶν γένος, ἐκ μιᾶς δὲ πνέομεν
        (Cretic)   (Cretic) echo

Glyconic   Glyconic

ματρὸς ἀμφότεροι· διείργει δὲ πᾶσα κεκριμένα
(Tripody)   (Tripody)
Aeol. tripody   Repeat

δύναμις, ὡς τὸ μὲν οὐδέν, ὁ δὲ χάλκεος ἀσφαλὲς αἰὲν ἕδος
                           Anapaests...

    μένει οὐρανός. ἀλλά τι προσφέρομεν ἔμπαν ἢ μέγαν
                        Epitrites

νόον ἤτοι φύσιν ἀθανάτοις,
Anap. Prosodiac

καίπερ ἐφαμερίαν οὐκ εἰδότες οὐδὲ μετὰ νύκτα
Prosodiac   Prosodiac   Epitrite

                   Glyconic

ἄμμε πότμος ἄντιν' ἔγραψē δραμέμεν ποτὶ στάθμαν.
Epitrite   Prosodiac

Ep.

                    Paeon

ἴχνεσιν ἐν Πραξιδάμαντος ἐὸν πόδα νέμων
Prosodiac   Prosodiac

Glyconic

πᾱτροπάτορος ὁμαιμίοις. κεῖνος γὰρ Ὀλυμπιόνικος ἐὼν Αἰακίδαις
                  Prosodiac   Prosodiac

           Aeol. tripody

ἔρνεα πρῶτος ἔνεικεν ἀπ' Ἀλφεοῦ,
Prosodiac

καὶ πεντάκις Ἰσθμοῖ στεφανωσάμενος,
Prosodiac   Prosodiac

Link   Dochmiac   Bacch.   Aeol. tripody

Νεμέᾳ δὲ τρεῖς, ἔπαυσε λάθαν Σαοκλείδα' ὃς ὑπέρτατος
                              echo

Ἀγησιμάχῳ ὑέων γένετο.
Prosodiac

The Glyconics at the beginning of the strophe are resumed in
the Glyconic at the end of the strophe; the bacchius followed

by a Glyconic at the beginning of the strophe is resumed in
the bacchius followed by an Aeolian tripody in the last phrase
but one of the epode. This gives the composition a loose three-
part form: in the strophe, Aeolian—Dorian—Aeolian, in the
epode Dorian—Aeolian—Dorian, with Paeonic as a recurrent
motive throughout.

O. v. Triadic: Dorian and dochmiac.

Str.

Prosodiac	Link (Pherecratic)

ὑψηλᾶν ἀρετᾶν καὶ στεφάνων ἄωτον γλυκὺν

Dochmiac

Prosodiac	Epitrite

τῶν Οὐλυμπίᾳ, Ὠκεανοῦ θύγατερ, καρδίᾳ γελανεῖ

ἀκαμαντόποδός τ' ἀπήνας δέκευ Ψαύμιός τε δῶρα.

Link (anapaests)	Dochmiac	Epitrite

Ep.

Prosodiac	Epitrite

ἵπποις ἡμιόνοις τε μοναμπυκίᾳ τε. τὶν δὲ κῦδος ἁβρὸν

Prosodiac

νικάσαις ἀνέθηκε καὶ ὃν πατέρ' Ἄκρων'

ἐκάρυξε καὶ τὰν νέοικον ἕδραν.

Dochmiac	Epitrite

Both strophe and epode end with the same dochmiac-epitrite
phrase, which has been anticipated in the strophe by ἄωτον
γλυκὺν and by καρδίᾳ γελανεῖ, in the epode by τὶν δὲ κῦδος
ἁβρόν.

P. ii. Triadic: Aeolian and Paeonic, with variations.

Str.

Trochaic

μεγαλοπόλιες ὦ Συράκοσαι, βαθυπολέμου

Pherecratic	Pherecratic	Tripody

τέμενος Ἄρεος, ἀνδρῶν ἵππων τε σιδαροχαρμᾶν δαιμόνιαι τροφοί,

Anapaests

ὕμμιν τόδε τὰν λιπαρᾶν ἀπὸ Θηβᾶν φέρων

Anapaests

μέλος ἔρχομαι ἀγγελίαν τετραορίας ἐλελίχθονος,

Trochaic-choriambic
_____
εὐάρματος Ἱέρων ἐν ᾆ κρατέων

Trochaic-choriambic
_____
τηλαυγέσιν ἀνέδησεν Ὀρτυγίαν στεφάνοις,

Tripody
_____
ποταμίας ἔδος Ἀρτέμιδος, ἃς οὐκ ἄτερ
                        Paeon   Cretic

Tripody   Trochaic-choriambic
_____
κείνας ἀγαναῖσιν ἐν χερσὶ ποικιλανίους ἐδάμασσε πώλους.
                                              Pherecratic

Ep.

Glyconic   Tripody
_____
ἱερέα κτίλον Ἀφροδίτας· ἄγει δὲ χάρις

Glyconic   Tripody
_____
φίλων ποί τινος ἀντὶ ἔργων ὀπιζομένα·

Glyconic   Tripody
_____
σὲ δ᾽, ὦ Δεινομένειε παῖ, Ζεφυρία πρὸ δόμων

Glyconic   Tripody   Trochaic
_____
Λοκρὶς παρθένος ἀπύει, πολεμίων καμάτων ἐξ ἀμαχάνων

Tripody   Dochmiac
_____
διὰ τεὰν δύναμιν δρακεῖσ᾽ ἀσφαλές.

Dochmiac   Pherecratic + iambus
_____
θεῶν δ᾽ ἐφετμαῖς Ἰξίονα φαντὶ ταῦτα βροτοῖς
                        (Dochmiac)

Pherecratic + iambus   Tripody
_____
λέγειν ἐν πτερόεντι τρόχῳ παντᾷ κυλινδόμενον·

Glyconic   Glyconic
_____
τὸν εὐεργέταν ἀγαναῖς ἀμοιβαῖς ἐποιχομένους τίνεσθαι.
                                    Pherecratic

A difficult piece, but interesting. The design is held together
by the Pherecratics: at the beginning of the strophe we have
two Pherecratics, at the end a Pherecratic cadence, and the
same arrangement is repeated in the epode. But the point of
the piece lies in the gradual emergence, both in strophe and
in epode, of Paeonic.

We begin with a long trochaic phrase: cf. *P.* vii 1 κάλλιστον αἱ μεγαλοπόλιες 'Αθᾶναι. I call it trochaic, but βαθυπολέμου may stand for a choriambus, anticipating ᾇ κρατέων and 'Ορτυγίαν. It is impossible to decide without the music. Then come two Pherecratics, the second with anacrusis, and an Aeolian tripody. The second Pherecratic is now taken up by anapaests, which lead to a short phrase ἀπὸ Θηβᾶν φέρων—a dochmiac all but for one short syllable. We return to anapaests, and then, after a figure in which anapaests are mixed with iambi, we hear a longish figure which seems to echo the trochaic phrase with which we began: for the sake of a name, I call it trochaic-choriambic. It is repeated; notice in both cases the hint of Paeonic— -ος Ἱέρων, -σιν ἀνέδη-. After a reminiscence of the anapaests heard above, we go on to a tripody, with the first foot resolved (ποταμίας). Repeat this effect, and you get a paeon, and again a cretic. We have arrived at Paeonic. Then another tripody; and then, for the third time, that trochaic-choriambic figure, running into the Pherecratic cadence.

The epode begins with a Glyconic followed by a tripody. Notice again that the first foot of the Glyconic is resolved (ἱερέα). Repeat both figures, this time transforming ἱερέα still further into φίλων ποί. Repeat again, and this time resolve the tripody (Ζεφυρία); repeat, and add ἐξ ἀμαχάνων—a trochaic figure which is often used as a form of the dochmiac (see Appendix). The tripody is repeated in its resolved form, and at last Paeonic re-emerges in two dochmiac figures. Then a Pherecratic followed by an iambus (the same phrase played a similar part in the First Olympian: see p. 76); this is repeated (in anaclastic form to remind us of Paeonic), then we get a tripody. Finally, the opening of the strophe is recalled by a Glyconic (again anaclastic); this is repeated and runs into the Pherecratic cadence.

6. Euripides, *Alcestis.*

The Aeschylean Chorus plays an integral part in the drama—hence the long choral odes, with their elaborate and highly dramatic organisation. Sophocles uses his Chorus for the same purpose, but less obviously: he maintains the technique of the recurrent leit-motive, but his odes tend to be shorter, less dynamic, more self-contained. In Euripides the Aeschylean tradition is beginning to weaken. The part played by the Chorus is relatively unimportant, and in many plays his odes are not interconnected as the successive movements of a single musical unity—they are more in the nature of musical *entr'actes*, both in form and in subject-matter, though, within these limits, as we have seen, he makes frequent use of strict strophic form and of significant rhythm. There are, in fact, two tendencies discernible in the work of this poet: one is the continuance of the Aeschylean convention—weaker, it is true, and more lax both in phrasing and in composition, but still quite clearly in the old tradition; the other is a new departure, in which he is the forerunner of Timotheus. The first may be illustrated from his earliest extant tragedy—the *Alcestis*.

The leading themes of the play are epitomised in the first strophe (86–97):

κλύει τις ἢ στεναγμὸν ἢ χειρῶν κτύπον κατὰ στέγας
Iambic

ἢ γόον ὡς πεπραγμένων;
Glyconic

Iambic and Glyconic—both themes will be developed. Then we have a run of dactylic (89–90)—this too is important. At 90–1 (εἰ γὰρ μετακύμιος ἄτας) the dactyls turn into anapaests, and at 93 the anapaestic movement is interrupted for a moment in order to introduce a passing allusion to Ionic a minore (νέκυς ἤδη, echoing ἐσιώπων). The second strophe introduces dochmiac and trochaic—both natural developments of iambic:

ἀλλ' οὐδὲ ναυκληρίαν ἔσθ' ὅποι τις αἴας . . .

After a couple of dactylic phrases and an echo (116 Ἀμμωνιάδας echoing ἐπὶ τὰς ἀνύδρους) we get a Pherecratic, and then a resumption of the opening of the first strophe:

ψυχάν· μόρος γὰρ ἀπότομος πλάθει, θεῶν δ᾽ ἐπ᾽ ἐσχάραις
Iambic

Finally, an Aeolian tripody brings the strophe to a close with a repetition of the Pherecratic cadence.

The first strophe of the second lyrical scene (213–71) resumes the dochmiac, iambic, trochaic and Glyconic motives:

ἰὼ Ζεῦ, τίς ἂν πᾷ πόρος κακῶν
Dochmiac

γένοιτο καὶ λύσις τύχας ἃ πάρεστι κοιράνοις;
Iambic   Trochaic

αἰαῖ· εἰσί τις, ἢ τέμω τρίχα,
Glyconic

καὶ μέλανα στολμὸν πέπλων ἀμφιβαλώμεθ᾽ ἤδη;
Glyconic[1]   Pherecratic

Dochmiac and iambic return, and the Pherecratic cadence:

δῆλα μὲν φίλοι, δῆλά γ᾽, ἀλλ᾽ ὅμως
Dochmiac

θεοῖσιν εὐχώμεσθα· θεῶν γὰρ δύναμις μεγίστα.
Iambic[2]   Pherecratic

Iambic returns at 222, then we hear a suggestion of dactylic (λυτήριος ἐκ θανάτου γενοῦ), leading to the third and final Pherecratic cadence: φόνιον δ᾽ ἀπόπαυσον Ἀίδαν.

The second strophe is a short one, but it has a beautiful cadence:

                    Pherecratic
Ἄλιε καὶ φάος ἀμέρας, οὐράνιαί τε δῖναι νεφέλας δρομαίου.
Enneasyllable   Pherecratic

The third begins with an echo of the first:

ὁρῶ δίκωπον ὁρῶ σκάφος ἐν λίμνᾳ· νεκύων δὲ πορθμεὺς . . .
=λυτήριος ἐκ θανάτου   Pherecratic

[1] A Glyconic, in spite of στολμόν: cf. 229 βρόχῳ. The licence is characteristic of Euripides: *Ion* 1229, *Supp.* 1001, 1005–7, *H. F.* 366.

[2] This figure sounds more like dochmiac, but the corresponding figure in the antistrophe (232) is iambic.

This echo is combined, in ὁρῶ δίκωπον, with an anticipation of the return to iambic which follows immediately:

ἔχων χέρ᾽ ἐπὶ κοντῷ Χάρων μ᾽ ἤδη καλεῖ, τί μέλλεις;

τί μέλλεις is echoed (ἐπείγου), and so leads to another touch of Ionic a minore before we return to the Pherecratic cadence:

σὺ κατείργεις. τάδε τοί με σπερχόμενος ταχύνει.
Ionic a minore   Pherecratic

The epode (266–71) reintroduces trochaic, with a touch of dactylic (πλησίον Ἀΐδας echoed in οὐκέτι μάτηρ σφῷν ἔστιν) and an unorthodox figure σκοτία δ᾽ ἐπ᾽ ὄσσοισι νὺξ ἐφέρπει, which seems to combine an echo of the trochaic we have already heard with an anticipation of the concluding figure of the scene:

χαίροντες, ὦ τέκνα, τόδε φάος ὁρῶτον.
Pherecratic

The next lyrical piece (393–415) begins by repeating 212–13:

ἰώ μοι τύχας. μαῖα δὴ κάτω βέβακεν, οὐκέτ᾽ ἔστιν, ὦ
Dochmiac   Iambic
          Pherecratic

πάτερ, ὑφ᾽ ἁλίῳ. προλιποῦσα δ᾽ ἁμὸν βίον ὠρφάνισσε τλάμων.
Dochmiac   Anacreontic

This Anacreontic, introduced by a shift which gives us a hint of Pherecratic, is a new motive. We return to dochmiac[1], then, with another shift (ὑπάκουσον ἄκουσον ὦ) to trochaic, Glyconic, and the Pherecratic cadence:

μᾶτερ, ἀντιάζω. ἐγώ σ᾽ ἐγώ, μᾶτερ,
Trochaic   Dochmiac

καλοῦμαί σ᾽ ὁ σὸς ποτὶ σοῖσι πίτνων στόμασιν νεοσσός.
Glyconic   Pherecratic

Next (435–75) we have a stasimon, and the rhythm changes to Dorian—a development of the dactylic phrases scattered through the earlier scenes, while the trochaics are now taken

---

[1] 399 βλέφαρον should be βλέφαρα.

up as epitrites. But the austerity of Dorian rhythm is tempered with several touches of the tender Anacreontic[1], and with a Pherecratic cadence:

Prosodiacs
—————————————————
ὦ Πελίου θύγατερ, χαίρουσά μοι εἰν Ἀίδαο δόμοις
Anacreontic
τὸν ἀνάλιον οἶκον οἰκετεύοις.

Prosodiacs
—————————————————
ἴστω δ' Ἀίδας ὁ μελαγχαίτας θεὸς ὅς τ' ἐπὶ κώπᾳ
Prosodiac   Epitrite
πηδαλίῳ τε γέρων νεκροπομπὸς ἵζει,
Anacreontic
πολὺ δὴ πολὺ δὴ γυναῖκ' ἀρίσταν
Anacreontic
λίμναν Ἀχερουτίαν πορεύσας ἐλάτᾳ δικώπῳ.
          Pherecratic

The second strophe begins where the last ended—with Pherecratic, which works, first by anaclasis, then by anacrusis, to a suggestion of Paeonic:

Pherecratic   with anaclasis
—————————————————
εἴθ' ἐπ' ἐμοὶ μὲν εἴη, δυναίμαν δέ σε πέμψαι
with anacrusis
φάος ἐξ Ἀίδα τεράμνων καὶ Κωκυτοῖο ῥεέθρων
Paeon   Trochaic
ποταμίᾳ νερτέρᾳ τε κώπᾳ.

The touches of Anacreontic return—between them, this time, is an Ionic a minore (σὺ τὸν αὐτᾶς); then we shift, through spondaic, to dactylic, the trochaic phrase is repeated (μάλ' ἂν ἔμοιγ' ἂν εἴη), and the strophe concludes with a touch of dochmiac (στυγηθεὶς τέκνοις τε τοῖς σοῖς), in fulfilment of the promise contained in δυναίμαν...ποταμίᾳ.

The next stasimon (569–605) begins in Dorian like the last,

[1] Cf. Aesch. P. V. 562–3 (p. 134), also Simon. 5, 1 ἄνδρ' ἀγαθὸν μὲν ἀλαθέως γενέσθαι, Bacchyl. xvii, 4 σάλπιγξ πολεμηίαν ἀοιδάν.

148 SUPPLEMENTARY NOTES

some of the same phrases being repeated, but its main function is to reintroduce Aeolian:

ἔτλα δὲ σοῖσι μηλονόμας ἐν δόμοις γενέσθαι,
<u>Glyconic</u>   <u>Trochaic</u>

δοχμιᾶν διὰ κλιτύων βοσκήμασι σοῖσι συρίζων
<u>Glyconic</u>   <u>See footnote[1]</u>

ποιμνίτας ὑμεναίους.
<u>Pherecratic</u>

The first strophe of the κομμός (861–933) is in the usual dochmiac; but the Aeolian motive is still maintained (876–7):

Glyconic
τὸ μήποτ᾽ εἰσιδεῖν φιλίας ἀλόχου πρόσωπον . . .
      <u>Pherecratic</u>

The second strophe is somewhat unorthodox: it is composed of fragmentary echoes of almost all the themes we have heard in the earlier odes, ending with an Ionian cadence like that in Aesch. *Agam.* 147 (p. 105). The short phrases, if somewhat irregular, are not inappropriate to the emotional tone of the words, which is personal, pathetic—a new note in Greek tragedy:

ἐμοί τις ἦν ἐν γένει, ᾧ κόρος ἀξιόθρηνος ὤλετ᾽ ἐν δόμοισιν
<u>Iambic</u>   <u>Dactylic</u>   <u>Trochaic</u>

μονόπαις· ἀλλ᾽ ἔμπας ἔφερε κακὸν ἅλις, ἄτεκνος ὤν,
<u>Ionic a minore?</u>   <u>Glyconic resolved</u>

πολιὰς ἐπὶ χαίτας ἤδη προπετὴς ὢν βιότου τε πόρσω.
<u>Ionic a minore</u>   <u>Cadence</u>

Passing on to the final stasimon (962–1005), we find that the Glyconics and Pherecratics which we have heard at frequent intervals ever since that initial ἢ γόον ὡς πεπραγμένων reach their consummation at last in a passage of continuous Aeolian:

ἐγὼ καὶ διὰ μούσας καὶ μετάρσιος ᾖξα, καὶ
πλείστων ἁψάμενος λόγων κρεῖσσον οὐδὲν ἀνάγκας . . .

1 A protracted Pherecratic? or is it yet another Euripidean variant of the Glyconic, with a spondee instead of a trochee in the third foot? Cf. *Hipp.* 141, 143–4, *Hec.* 469–71, *El.* 116.

On the whole, therefore, we may say that this, the earliest of the extant tragedies of Euripides, has yielded to the methods of analysis which we applied to the plays of Aeschylus, though the dramatic organisation is less highly developed, and here and there we have come across phrases which might have prompted the older poet to protest.

Euripides never abandoned the old convention entirely: many examples have been quoted in previous chapters from his plays, both early and late, in which he uses significant rhythm and strophic form hardly less effectively than his predecessor. But along with this maintenance of the Aeschylean tradition it is possible to trace the beginnings of a new development, particularly in his monodies—that feature of his later style which Aristophanes singled out for his shafts of good-humoured ridicule.

Hel. 241–8

ἃ δὲ χρυσέοις θρόνοις Διὸς ὑπαγκάλισμα σεμνὸν
Ἥρα τὸν ὠκύπουν ἔπεμψε Μαιάδος γόνον·
ὅς με χλοερὰ δρεπομέναν ἔσω πέπλων ῥόδεα πέταλα,
Χαλκίοικον ὡς μόλοιμ᾽, ἀναρπάσας δι᾽ αἰθέρος
τάνδε γαῖαν εἰς ἄνολβον ἔριν ἔριν τάλαιναν ἔθετο
Πριαμίδαισιν Ἑλλάδος.

This is not difficult to analyse—it is a very simple composition in trochaic and iambic. But rhythmically it is dull: it has none of the flexibility and subtlety with which Aeschylus and Pindar wove their masterly designs. That is not because Euripides was a duller artist—he could weave as beautiful a design as any when he chose to do so: but here he is attempting something different. It is clear that the point of this passage, and of others like it, does not lie in the rhythm; it seems probable that it lay in the lost melody which accompanied it.

As Pratinas perceived, the danger-point lay in such performances as the hyporcheme and dithyramb, where there were no dramatic requirements, insisting on the supremacy of the words, to hold the innovating musician in check. The Euripidean monody belongs to this class. Its function is merely to express a mood, or to provide an appropriate setting for a song or dance. There is little dramatic significance in the words, and hence no rhythmical elaboration is required to bring it out. Accordingly, in these extravaganzas Euripides abandons the old rhythmical conventions in order to give scope to what must have been the central feature of such performances—the new experiments in melody and choreography.

Or. 1381–92

Ἴλιον, Ἴλιον, ὤμοι μοι,

Φρύγιον ἄστυ καὶ καλλίβωλον Ἴδας ὄρος ἱερόν, ὥς σ᾽ ὀλόμενον
 στένω

βαρβάρῳ βοᾷ δι᾽ ὀρνιθόγονον

ὄμμα κυκνοπτέρου καλλοσύνας, Λήδας σκύμνου, δυσελένας,
 δυσελένας,

ξεστῶν περγάμων Ἀπολλωνίων

ἐρινύν· ὀττοτοῖ· ἰαλέμων ἰαλέμων

Δαρδανίᾳ τλᾶμον Γανυμήδεος ἱπποσύνᾳ Διὸς εὐνέτα.

Here and there we hear an echo of standard phrases, but in general it is plain that the old principles, both of phrasing and of composition, have broken down.

Timotheus, *Persae* 26–31

στερεοπαγῆ δ᾽ ἐφέρετο φόνια μόλιβα πισσάεντά τε περίβολα
 πυρὶ φλεγόμεν᾽ ἐν ἀποτομάσι βουδόροις,

ὄφεσι δὲ βίοτος ἐθύετ᾽ ἀδινὸς ὑπὸ τανυπτέροισι χαλκόκρασι
 νευροπεντάτοις.

Here the revolution is complete: poetical beauty and rhythmical subtlety, at least in so far as it was wedded to the words, have been thrown to the winds, and we are left with a mere operatic *libretto*. In the words of Timotheus himself (he seems to revive for a moment the dying convention in order to point the contrast)[1]:

οὐκ ἀείδω τὰ παλαιά, καινὰ γὰρ μάλα κρείσσω·
νέος ὁ Ζεὺς βασιλεύει, τὸ πάλαι δ᾽ ἦν Κρόνος ἄρχων·
ἀπίτω Μοῦσα παλαιά.

---

[1] *fr.* 14.

APPENDIX

Appended is (1) a summary of the standard phrases in each class of rhythm, together with variants and rare forms not mentioned in Chapter II; and (2) a list of further examples in illustration of the metrical principles formulated in Chapters IV–V.

I. DORIAN.

The normal figures are:

(1) Prosodiac: ‒⏑⏑ ‒⏑⏑ ‒(‒)

‒⏑⏑ ‒⏑⏑ ‒⏑⏑ ‒(‒)

‒⏑⏑ ‒(‒)

The first two forms require no illustration. For the third, cf. Pind. *P.* iv 20 ματρόπολιν Θή-: Soph. *Aj.* 181 -τείσατο λώβαν: *O. C.* 1090 Παλλὰς Ἀθάνα: Pind. *N.* viii 2 -α γλεφάροις: 16 -ων σταδίων: xi 5 οἵ σε γεραί-: Aesch. *Supp.* 43 ἀνθονομού-.

(2) Epitrite: ‒⏑ ‒‒

‒⏑ ‒

‒⏑ ‒⏑ ‒‒

‒‒⏑‒

For the third of these forms (not used by Pindar or Bacchylides) cf. Simon. 57, 6 φωτὸς ἅδε βουλά: Aesch. *P. V.* 551 μήποτ᾽ ἐκτακείη: *Supp.* 92–3 κἂν σκότῳ μελαίνᾳ. For the fourth, cf. Pind. *N.* i 72 δαίσαντα πὰρ, Simon. 37, 9 ἄλμαν δ᾽ ὕπερ-, Soph. *Aj.* 221 οἵαν ἐδή-, *O. T.* 863 εἴ μοι ξυνεί-, *O. C.* 1090 σεμνά τε παῖς, Eur. *I. T.* 1234 εὔπαις ὁ Λα-, *Rh.* 224 Θυμβραῖε καὶ, 363 ψαλμοῖσι καὶ.

Anacrusis.

(1) Single (⏑ or ‒). In prosodiac: Pind. *O.* iii 3 Θήρωνος Ὀλυμπιονίκαν: *N.* v 13 ὁ τᾶς θεοῦ ὃν Ψαμάθεια. In epitrite: Pind. *I.* i 5 τί φίλτερον κεδ-: *O.* viii 22 πάρεδρος ἀσκεῖ-: 44 πεμφθὲν βαρυγδού-.

(2) Double (⏑⏑). Only in prosodiac: Pind. *P.* iii 23 μετάμωνια θηρεύ-: Arist. Bergk II pp. 360–2 Ἀρετὰ πολύμοχθε γε-.

Resolution.

(1) Of prosodiac: Pind. *I.* iv 45 ‒⏑⏑ ⏑⏑⏑⏑ ‒‒ ἐρνεΐ Τελεσιάδα τόλ-. Long dactylic phrases obtained by resolution of the final spondee:

Pind. *P.* iii 4 Οὐρανίδα γόνον εὐρυμέδοντα Κρόνου : Soph. *Aj.* 172 ἦ ῥά σε Ταυροπόλα Διὸς Ἄρτεμις, ὦ μεγάλα φάτις ὦ : *O. T.* 151–2 ὦ Διὸς ἁδυεπὲς Φάτι, τίς ποτε τᾶς πολυχρύσου : Aesch. *Supp.* 45–6 Ζηνός· ἔφαψιν ἐπωνυμίᾳ δ᾽ ἐπεκραίνετο μόρσιμος αἰών : Eur. *Andr.* 117 ὦ γύναι, ἃ Θέτιδος δάπεδον καὶ ἀνάκτορα θάσσεις. This is the origin of the long dactylic phrases of Stesichorus (see pp. 103–4).

(2) Of epitrite : ᵕᵕᵕ ‒⌣‒ Pind. *O.* xi 15 Ζεφυρίων Λοκ- : *P.* i 17 Κιλίκιον θρέ-. ᵕᵕᵕ ‒⌣ Pind. *P.* i 15 πολέμιος : *I.* ii 15 -εν ἀναδεῖσ-. ‒⌣ ᵕᵕ‒ Pind. *I.* iv 54 b -ωνος ἐρέφον-. ‒⌣ ‒⌣ᵕᵕ Simon. 4, 5 οὔθ᾽ ὁ πανδαμά- : Aesch. *Supp.* 47–8 εὐλόγως Ἐπα- : *ibid.* 93–4 ξὺν τίχᾳ μερό-.

Substitution.

(1) In prosodiac : trochee for final spondee : Pind. *P.* iv 4 ἔνθα ποτὲ χρυσέων Διὸς αἰε- : *N.* v 2 ὁλκάδος ἔν τ᾽ ἀκάτῳ γλυ- : *O.* viii 17 Ἀλκιμέδοντα δὲ πὰρ Κρο- : Soph. *Ant.* 582 εὐδαίμονες οἷσι κακῶν ἄ-.

(2) In epitrite : trochee for final spondee : Pind. *P.* iv 5 -ος τυχόντες : *ibid.* 23 δέξατ᾽ αἰσί-.

Anaclasis.

The following irregular openings in Pindar are perhaps due to anaclasis :

⌣‒‒ (for ‒⌣‒?) : Pind. *O.* vi 6 συνοικισ-.
⌣⌣‒‒ (for ‒⌣⌣‒?) : Pind. *O.* vii 1 φιάλαν ὥς, cf. 7, 18 (see p. 57) : viii 6 ἀρετὰν θυ- : *P.* i 20 νιφόεσσ᾽ Αἴτ- : ix 1 ἐθέλω χαλ-. From this variant we get by substitution ⌣⌣‒⌣ Pind. *P.* ix 3 Τελεσίκρά-. There is a still further variant ⌣⌣‒ in *N.* viii 13 ἱκέτας.

Protraction.

Of epitrite : Stesich. 32, 2 ναυσὶν εὐσέλμοις, Aesch. *Supp.* 48 -ον τ᾽ ἐγέννασε, Soph. *Aj.* 602 αἰὲν εὐνῶμαι, *O. T.* 1097 ταῦτ᾽ ἀρέστ᾽ εἴη, *O. C.* 1085–6 -αρχε παντόπτα.

II. IONIAN.

(1) Ionic a minore : ⌣⌣‒‒.

Variants, by substitution : ‒⌣‒ Sappho 62 κατθνάσκει, Soph. *Aj.* 629 οὐδ᾽ οἰκτρᾶς. ⌣⌣‒⌣⌣ Aesch. *Pers.* 97 -ματος εὐπετέ-, Eur. *Bacch.* 522 τὸ Διὸς βρέφος.

Variants, by anaclasis : ‒⌣‒⌣ Aesch. *Supp.* 1032 -ιν παλαιόν, *Pers.* 953–4 -φρακτος Ἄρης, *P. V.* 421 -νυσιν αἰχμήν.

Continuous Ionic a minore often contains occasional anapaests or spondees, and bacchii: Eur. *Bacch.* 64–167, 370–432, 519–75, *passim*; Soph. *El.* 829 ὦ παῖ, Eur. *Phoen.* 1539–42. The usual cadences are Anacreontic (Aesch. *Supp.* 1036, 1053) and ‿‿⏒‿⏒‿ (Eur. *Bacch.* 385 ὕπνον ἀμφιβάλλῃ, the latter being commonly taken in conjunction with the preceding phrase to suggest, by overlap, a Pherecratic (p. 105).

(2) Anacreontic: ‿‿⏒‿‿⏒‿‿ obtained from Ionic a minore by anaclasis (see p. 8).

(3) Choriambic: ⏒‿‿⏒. Variants: ⏒–⏒ Soph. *El.* 473–4 καὶ γνώμας: ⏒‿‿‿⏒ Anacr. 24 ἀναπέτομαι.
Choriambic phrases often have a spondee or trochee prefixed: Alcaeus 37 A, 41, Soph. *El.* 473: and very commonly they pass by overlap into a Pherecratic or Aeolian tripody: Alcaeus 37 A, 41, Anacreon 22–5, 28.

(4) Iambo-choriambic: ‿⏒‿⏒ ⏒‿‿⏒ obtained from choriambic by anaclasis (see p. 9). We also find –‿⏒‿⏒ ⏒‿‿⏒ Aesch. *P. V.* 130 μηδὲν φοβηθῇς· φιλία, and ‿⏒–⏒ ⏒‿‿⏒ Eur. *Supp.* 975 ἀοιδαί θ᾽ ἃς χρυσοκόμας, and –⏒–⏒ ⏒‿‿⏒ Eur. *Hel.* 1316 ἔγχει Γοργῶπις πάνοπλος.

(5) There are a number of other phrases which may be conveniently classified as Ionian. Some of them, in which anapaests and iambics are combined, seem to be developments of the Anacreontic.

‿‿⏒ ‿⏒ ‿⏒ Eur. *Hipp.* 125 ὅθι μοί τις ἦν φίλα.
‿‿⏒ ‿⏒ ‿⏒ ‿⏒– Pind. *O.* ix 22 μαλεραῖς ἐπιφλέγων ἀοιδαῖς, iv 8, *N.* vi 20.
⏓⏒ ‿‿⏒ ‿⏒ At beginning of strophe Pind. *O.* ix 1 τὸ μὲν Ἀρχιλόχου μέλος, Soph. *O. T.* 1186, *O. C.* 1044–6, Eur. *Hec.* 466–7, *Supp.* 778, *El.* 167; elsewhere Ar. *Eq.* 1111–30, Soph. *Ant.* 612, *O. T.* 467–8, Eur. *Ion* 468–9.
⏓⏒‿‿⏒‿⏒‿⏒– Eur. *Alc.* 437 τὸν ἀνάλιον οἶκον οἰκετεύοις, *ibid.* 442, 460, *Hipp.* 526–8, *Hec.* 927, *Rh.* 900–1, Pind. *I.* vii 1.
‿‿⏒ ‿⏒ ‿‿⏒– Pind. *O.* iv 1 ἐλατὴρ ὑπέρτατε βροντᾶς.

III. AEOLIAN.

(1) Glyconic: ⏒⏑ ⏒‿‿ ⏒‿ ⏒. The dactyl normally occupies second place, but is often found in first or third. The substitution of spondees for trochees is Euripidean (pp. 145 n., 148 n.). Resolution

is common in the first and second feet: Pind. *N.* vii 21 λόγον Ὀδυσσέος ἢ πάθαν, Soph. *Trach.* 947 πότερα πρότερον ἐπιστένω: in the third, Pind. *P.* v 32 -θεὶς γέρας ἀμφέβαλε τεαῖ-: in the fourth, Eur. *Hipp.* 146 = 156 -τας ἔξορμος ἀνὴρ λιμένα, *Hec.* 452 καλλίστων ὑδάτων πατέρα, *Bacch.* 910 τὸ δὲ κατ᾽ ἦμαρ ὅτῳ βίοτος: in all four, *Hel.* 1308 κρόταλα δὲ βρόμια διαπρύσιον. Also, an anapaest is found in place of the initial spondee in a few cases, Soph. *O. C.* 704, Eur. *ap.* Ar. *Ran.* 1322 (see p. 65): cf. *Hel.* 1314 μετὰ κούραν, ἀελλόποδες. By anaclasis we get the common form ◡⏑ ⏑◡◡ ◡◡ ⏑.

(2) Pherecratic: ⏑◡ ◡◡⏑ ⏑– and ◡⏑⏑ ◡⏑ ⏑–. The first trochee is often resolved, sometimes in order to suggest Paeonic: Pind. *O.* i 28 b φάτις ὑπὲρ τὸν ἀλαθῆ. Resolution in third foot: Pind. *N.* vii 17 -οντα τριταῖον ἄνεμον (p. 45: but perhaps this is iambo-choriambic followed by a fourth paeon). There is also a protracted form: Soph. *Trach.* 949 δύσκριτ᾽ ἔμοιγε δυστάνῳ, *Ant.* 816, 846, *Aj.* 1191, and an anaclastic form: Pind. *O.* i 24 ἐν εὐάνορι Λυδοῦ, Anacr. 16, 2, Eur. *H. F.* 390, *Ion* 1080, 1089, Soph. *Phil.* 1125.

(3) Tripody: ⏑◡ ◡◡⏑ ⏑ and ◡◡⏑ ◡◡ ⏑.

(4) Enneasyllables: ⏑◡ ◡◡⏑ ◡◡ ⏑– Aesch. *Cho.* 386 πευκηέντ᾽ ὀλολυγμὸν ἀνδρός: ⏑◡◡ ◡◡⏑ ◡◡⏑ Eur. *Alc.* 244 Ἅλιε καὶ φάος ἀμέρας.

(5) Decasyllable: ⏑◡◡ ◡◡⏑ ◡◡ ⏑– Aesch. *P. V.* 135 κραιπνοφόροι δέ μ᾽ ἔπεμψαν αὖραι.

(6) Hendecasyllable: ⏑◡◡ ◡◡ ◡◡ ◡◡ ⏑– Pind. *N.* vii 2 παῖ μεγαλοσθενέος ἄκουσον Ἥρας.

(7) Heptasyllable: ⏑◡◡⏑ ◡◡⏑. This is not a standard phrase, but grows out of Glyconic by isolation of the choriambic and cretic elements in that phrase: Simon. 37, 14, Pind. *P.* x 2 (see p. 68).

IV. Paeonic:

(1) Simple Paeonic:

Cretic ⏑◡⏑, Bacchius ◡⏑–, First paeon ⏑◡◌◡, Fourth paeon ◌◡◡⏑, Palimbacchius –⏑◡ (Aesch. *Agam.* 153 Παιᾶνα, 1057 ὤπολλον ὤπολλον), and (if this foot is Paeonic) ⏑–⏑ Molottus (Soph. *O. C.* 121–2).

(2) Dochmiac (obtained by combination of the above feet with iambic):

"Slow" dochmiac: ⏑⸋–⏑⸋
           ⏑⸋⏑⸋–
           ⸋⏑⸋⏑⸋ (Pind. *O.* ii 16 ἐν δίκᾳ τε καὶ, Soph. *Aj.*
401–2, 403–5, *O. T.* 1208–11).

"Quick" dochmiac: ⸋⏑⏑⸋⏑⸋
           ⏑⸋⏑⏑⏑⸋.

By substitution ⸋⏑⏑⸋⏑⸋ gives ⸋⏑⏑⸋⏑⸋, by resolution ⏑⸋⏑⸋– gives
⏑⸋⏑⸋⏑⏑ (Soph. *O. C.* 702 τὸ μέν τις οὐ νεα-, Aesch. *Theb.* 508
πέποιθα τὸν Διὸς), by protraction ⏑⸋⏑⸋– gives ⏑⸋⏑⸋–– (Aesch. *Agam.*
207–8, see p. 108). A rare form of dochmiac (first paeon + iambic)
occurs in Aesch. *Theb.* 508 ἀντίτυπον ἔχοντ'.

The following figures also, as well as the simple Paeonic feet and
iambic figures, are found in continuous dochmiac composition:

⏑⏑⸋–– Aesch. *Cho.* 935 βαρύδικος Ποινά, Eur. *Bacch.* 1168 Ἀσιάδες
βάκχαι.

⏑⸋–– Aesch. *Agam.* 206 παλιμμηκῆ, 379 Διὸς πλαγάν.

⸋⏑⸋ Pind. *O.* ii 7 εὐωνύμων, Aesch. *Supp.* 569 Τυφῶ μένος.

–⸋–⏑– (for ⏑⸋–⏑⸋) Soph. *Ant.* 1311 δειλαίᾳ δὲ συγ-.

–⸋⏑⸋– (for ⏑⸋⏑⸋–) Pind. *O.* ii 3 ἤτοι Πίσα μέν.

TROCHAIC.

The common phrases are:

(1) ⸋⏑ ⸋⏑ ⸋⏑ ⸋
(2) ⸋⏑ ⸋⏑ ⸋–
(3) ⸋⏑ ⸋⏑ ⸋⏑ ⸋–
(4) ⸋⏑⸋ ⸋⏑ ⸋⏑ ⸋⏑ ⸋

The first of these is used by Alcman and by Pindar in Aeolian (see
p. 78). In continuous trochaic we often find a cretic variant ⸋⏑⸋ ⸋⏑⸋
(Aesch. *Agam.* 190 μνησιπήμων πόνος).

IAMBIC.

The common phrases are:

(1) ⏑⸋ ⏑⸋
(2) ⸋⸋ ⏑⸋ ⏑⸋–
(3) ⸋⸋ ⏑⸋ ⸋⸋ ⏑⸋
(4) the iambic trimeter.

There is another rhythm, ‑⌣⌣⌣‑, which does not fall readily into any of the above-mentioned classes, though it seems to have originated in the resolution of the common epitritic or dochmiac variant ‑‑⌣‑ : Pind. *O.* xiv 10 Πύθιον 'Απόλλ- (from 1 Καφισίων).

‑⌣⌣⌣‑ Aesch. *Theb.* 138 Ἄρτεμι φίλα, Soph. *Phil.* 201 εὔστομ' ἔχε, παῖ, 833 ὦ τέκνον, ὅρα, Pind. *fr.* 75. 5 εὐκλέ' ἀγοράν.

‑⌣⌣⌣‑⌣ Pind. *fr.* 76–77, 2 Ἑλλάδος ἔρεισμα.

‑⌣⌣⌣‑‑‑ Soph. *Phil.* 835 φροντίδος ὁρᾷς εὕδει.

‑⌣⌣⌣‑⌣‑ Pind. *fr.* 75, 2 πέμπετε χάριν θεοί.

Two-part Form.

For further examples of two-part form, see Eur. *Hipp.* 525–33 (A 525–9, B 530–3), *Supp.* 373–6 (A iambic, B Paeonic), 955–62 (A 955–7, B 958–62), *H. F.* 106–17 (A 106–12, B 113–17), 408–18 (A 408–11, B 412–18), Ar. *Ach.* 836–41.

Three-part Form.

For further examples of three-part form, see Soph. *O. T.* 151–9 (A...πολυχρύσου, B...ἔβας, A...πάλλων, C...Παιάν, A...χρέος, A...Φάμα), *Trach.* 132–40 (A Paeonic, B trochaic and iambic, A Paeonic), *Phil.* 169–79 (A Glyconic and Pherecratic, B 175–7, A Glyconic and Pherecratic), 827–38 (A 827, B spondaic, C ‑⌣⌣⌣‑, B spondaic, A 838), 1140–5 (1140 = 1145), *O. C.* 668–80 (668–9 = 678–9), 694–706 (694 = 706), Eur. *Andr.* 117–25 (A Dorian, B Paeonic, A Dorian), *H. F.* 348–58 (A Aeolian, B 352–3, A Aeolian), *Ion* 1229–43 (A Aeolian, B 1233–41, A Aeolian), *Tro.* 1060–70 (A Glyconic and Pherecratic, B 1066–70, A final Pherecratic), *Phoen.* 239–49 (A trochaic dimeters, B 246–8, A trochaic dimeter), *Bacch.* 105–19 (A Glyconic and Pherecratic, B Ionic a minore and dactylic, A Glyconic and Pherecratic), Ar. *Lys.* 321–34 (A iambo-choriambic and choriambic, B choriambic into Pherecratic, A iambo-choriambic and choriambic), *Plut.* 290–5, 316–21, *Ach.* 1008–17, Timocr. 1 (str., cf. epode), Pind. *O.* iii str. (A–B–A 1–3, C–D–C 4–5).

A looser variety of three-part form is obtained by making the closing cadence repeat a phrase which has· been heard already in the course of the early part of the design (see p. 85, n. 1): Aesch. *Theb.* 738 ὅστε ματρὸς ἀγνάν = 742 νυμφίους φρενώλεις, 818 γένεος Οἰδίπου τ' ἀρά = 824 -δε ξυναυλία δορός, Soph. *Aj.* 224 ἄτλατον οὐδὲ φευκτάν = 232 βοτῆρας

APPENDIX 157

ἱππονώμας, 598 πᾶσιν περίφαντος αἰεί = 607 τὸν ἀπότροπον ἀίδηλον Ἀίδαν, *El.* 505 πολύπονος ἱππεία = 515 πολύπονος αἰκεία, *O. T.* 464 Δελφὶς εἶπε πέτρα = 472 Κῆρες ἀναπλάκητοι, *Ant.* 606 τὰν οὔθ᾽ ὕπνος αἱρεῖ ποθ᾽ ὁ παντογήρως = 614 θνατῶν βιότῳ πάμπολύ γ᾽ ἐκτὸς ἄτας, Eur. *Hcld.* 354 σοῦ πλέον οὐ μέλονται = 361 -γει Σθενέλου τύραννος, 773 πόρευσον ἄλλᾳ τὸν οὐ δικαίως = 776 δίκαιός εἰμ᾽ ἐκπεσεῖν μελάθρων, *Hec.* 446 ἀκάτους ἐπ᾽ οἶδμα λίμνας = 454 -πιδανὸν πέδια λιπαίνειν, *Tro.* 521 ἐν πύλαις Ἀχαιοί = 530 δόλιον ἔσχον ἄταν, *Hel.* 1452 κώπα ῥοθίοισι ματήρ = 1464 οἴκων Ἑλέναν ἐπ᾽ ἀκταῖς, Alcman 23, 37 ὁ δ᾽ ὄλβιος ὅστις εὔφρων = 49 ὑποπετριδίων ὀνείρων.

Pindar gives unity to his strophe or epode, or binds strophe and epode together, in the same way; only with him the repetition often comes a little before the end of the design: *O.* iv 4 ἔσαναν αὐτίκ᾽ ἀγγελίαν = 24 νέοις ἐν ἀνδράσιν πολίαι, *O.* vii 1 φιάλαν ὡς = 7 πορευόντων = 18 Ἀσίας εὐ-, xiv 1 ταί τε ναίετε καλλίπωλον ἕδραν = 11 -βοντι πατρὸς Ὀλυμπίοιο τιμάν, *P.* ii 2 ἵππων τε σιδαροχαρμᾶν = 8 -νίους ἐδάμασσε πώλους = 24 ἐποιχομένους τίνεσθαι.

INDEX.

For EU product safety concerns, contact us at Calle de José Abascal, 56–1°, 28003 Madrid, Spain or eugpsr@cambridge.org.

www.ingramcontent.com/pod-product-compliance
Ingram Content Group UK Ltd.
Pitfield, Milton Keynes, MK11 3LW, UK
UKHW012342130625
459647UK00009B/460